MEAL PREP

KETO MEAL PREP

MEAL PREP

Table of Contents

KETO MEAL PREP

KETO MEAL PREP FOR BEGINNERS

INTRODUCTION

In The United States, the obesity epidemic continues to rise. 38% of our adult population are considered obese. Another 33% of persons are considered overweight. This is according to The Centers For Disease Control and Prevention.

The numbers are even higher for women. Women, because of our child-bearing bodies, have other factors we must contend with. Elevated estrogen levels and different female hormones have our bodies already at a higher fat percentage. Obesity is medically defined as having a body index (BMI) of more than 30%. Personally, I have dieted almost my entire adult life. I'm now over the age of 50. I began to look for a better way to approach fooA Ketogenic is a diet known as a very low carb diet. It is a high fat, moderate protein and low carb intake diet. It turns your body into a fat burning machine. There is a much more scientific explanation but basically you force your body to produce ketones in the liver to be used for energy. On the opposite end, eating foods high in carbs and sugars your body will produce glucose and raise insulin levels.

Although ketogenics is new to many, it was around as early as the 1920s. The keto lifestyle can have a healthful effect on serious health conditions, like cardiovascular diseases and diabetes. It improves levels of HDL cholesterol.

To enter into ketosis, you need to reduce your carbs to under 50 grams a day. Ideally 25-30 carbs max. Your fat intake should be about 75% of your meals and about 15% protein. It varies from person to person, but with consistency you should be able to get into ketosis within 3-14 days.

When you consume a high amount of carbohydrates your metabolism spends most of the time burning carbs for fuel. You never get to burn stored fat. If you decrease the amount of available carbs, your body must switch to burning your fat.

CHAPTER ONE

THE BASIC PRINCIPLES OF THE KETOGENIC DIET

The ketogenic diet is a diet based on a process called ketosis. It is a specific state of the body, which is characterized by an elevated level of ketones in the blood, which occurs due to the conversion of fats into fatty acids and ketones. This occurs when the body gets only very small amounts of carbohydrates over a certain period of time. When you start with this type of diet, your body goes through several changes. 24-48 hours after the beginning of this diet, the body starts to use ketones in order to use the energy stored in fat cells more efficiently. In other words, the primary source of energy becomes fat (fatty acids), instead of carbohydrates (glucose). Because of that, during ketosis it is not a problem to eat food with higher amounts of fat, than would otherwise seem reasonable. This way the body is rapidly losing weight (specifically fat). In addition, the loss of muscle tissue (proteins) is minimal, since the vast majority of food consumed during ketosis, also contains relatively large amounts of proteins that are good for your muscles.

Although ketosis is the basis of the ketogenic type of diet, in its strictest form it doesn't need to be kept for long. The state of ketosis can be held up until the body weight is just a few pounds higher than the one that is desired. Then foods with higher amounts of carbohydrates are gradually introduced (rice, beans). In this period, it would be very useful to keep a food intake diary in which daily amounts of taken carbs would be noted. That way you can find the maximum amount of daily carbs that still allow you not to gain weight. Once you discover this parameter, you will no longer have weight-related problems, because you will certainly learn to take account of the calories and amounts of carbs, proteins and fats that you consume daily. That way you will get to know your body better, in terms of the maximum "allowable" daily intake. Because of that, we could say that the ketogenic diet is, in a way, a procedure for learning habits that will ensure that you never return to the old potentially problematic overweight levels.

There are many types of ketogenic diets , but they all have in common one basic principle: the intake of high amounts of proteins and fats, and minimal amounts of carbohydrates. Which exact diet you will choose isn't as important, as long as it will allow you to enter ketosis, which is the basis of the biological mechanism that will help you lose weight efficiently.

Low carb diets have advantages and disadvatages.

The reason low carb has a bad rap is that people say they are low carb, but really aren't. It's like saying you're low calorie while eating a bowl of ice cream with a donut on top. The people who give low carb a bad name do not follow the basic principle of low carb: a constant, steady stream of carbs that have a total during the day of less than a set amount, usually 100g, and all of the carbs come from fruits and vegetables. Of course, some diets are more strict and I myself keep to below 70g per day.

So, who are these people who say they are low carb, but really aren't? Well, they starve themselves of carbs, focus on meats and fats only and then pig out on sugar on the weekends. Then they start all over again. These people are cranky, depressed and miserable. Plus, they aren't losing a pound. They blame the diet and not the dieter who isn't doing it right.

Doctors hate the low carb diet because of these people. You see, when you starve yourself of something, then pig out, you force your body to shift it's metabolism from ketogenic (protein) metabolism to carbohydrate metabolism quickly, and it doesn't like it. It leads to a stressed liver, heart and brain. It produces lots of cortisol, which causes us to hold onto fat and store even more. It layers plaque in our arteries to help reduce the stress. It harms the kidneys because of the toxic burden of switching back and forth.

The focus on meats and fats deprives the body of vital nutrients and the organs start to break down. This kind of dieting makes people sick. This is where many of the myths of the low carb diet come from: these people who are not doing low carb at all.

For those who want to do it right, it requires discipline. It requires long periods of constant, steady streams of carbs, without spikes or indulgences. In fact, it is one of the healthiest diets to be on. Lower carb is the basis of all healthy diets: Mediterranean, vegetarian, diabetic, Atkins and all the others.

BASIC PRINCIPLES OF THE KETOGENIC DIET

Doing it right goes like this:

Set your carbs: I recommend no less than 60g/day unless under the care of a nutritionist.

Plan your day around your fruits and vegetables: I recommend no less than 5 servings per day

Make sure those fruits and vegetables are within your carb counts.

Flavor with herbs and spices – as many as possible (they have 0 carbs!)

Fill in with local, organic or natural meats and healthy fats.

Planning this way will allow you to consume many foods, enough to keep you full and happy and provide all the nutrition you require.

There is only one problem with eating low carb the right way. Fruits and vegetables do not have convenient packages to know exactly how many carbs are in them. A pepper is usually about 6g per serving, but can be as low as 4g in the spring to nearly 10g in the fall. But that's OK, you don't need to be that precise, so long as fruits and vegetables make up the biggest part of your diet.

CHAPTER TWO

WHY KETO MEALS

Keto diets have really caught on in the past year and a half and for good reason. It's a great way to not only shed those unwanted pounds quickly, but also a great way to get healthy and stay that way. For those that have tried the Keto Diet and are still on it, it's more than just a diet. It's a way of life, a completely new lifestyle. But like any major shift in our lives it is not an easy one, and it takes an incredible amount of commitment and determination.

Good for some but not for all? Although a ketogenic diet has been used to greatly improve people's quality of life, there are some out there who do not share the majority's way of thinking. But why is that exactly? Ever since we can remember we have been taught that the only way to get rid of the extra weight was to quit eating the fat-filled foods that we are so accustomed to eating every day. So instructing people to eat healthy fats (the key word is healthy), you can certainly understand why some people would be skeptical as to how and why you would eat more fat to achieve weight loss and achieve it fast. This concept goes against everything we have ever known about weight loss.

How Keto Started. Discovered by endocrinologist Rollin Woodyatt in 1921 when he found that 3 water-soluble compounds named aceture, B-hydroxybutyrate and acetoacetate (known together as ketone bodies) were produced by the liver as a result of starvation or if the person followed a diet rich with high fat and very low carbs. Later on that year a man from the Mayo Clinic by the name of Russel Wilder named it the "Ketogenic Diet" and used it to treat epilepsy in young children with great success. But because of advancements in medicine it was replaced.

What Does A Ketogenic Diet Look Like? When the average person eats a meal rich in carbs, their body takes those carbs and converts them into glucose for fuel. Glucose is the body's main source of fuel when carbs are present in the body; on a keto diet there are very low if any carbs consumed which forces the body to utilize other forms of energy to keep the body functioning properly. This is where healthy fats come into play; with the absence of carbs the liver takes fatty acids in the body and converts them into ketone bodies.

An ideal keto diet should consist of:

- 70-80% Fat

- 20-25% Protein

- 5-10% Carbs

You should not be eating more than 20g of carbs per day to maintain the typical Ketogenic diet. I personally ate less than 10g per day for a more drastic experience but I achieved my initial goals and then some. I lost 28 lbs in a little under 3 weeks.

What Is Ketosis? When the body is fueled completely by fat it enters a state called "ketosis" which is a natural state for the body. After all of the sugars and unhealthy fats have been removed from the body during the first couple of weeks, the body is now free to run on healthy fats. Ketosis has many potential benefits related to rapid weight loss, health or performance. In certain situations like type 1 diabetes excessive ketosis can become extremely dangerous, whereas in certain cases paired with intermittent fasting it can be extremely beneficial for people suffering from type 2 diabetes. Substantial work is being conducted on this topic by Dr. Jason Fung M.D. (Nephrologist) of the Intensive Dietary Management Program.

What I Can and Can't Eat. For someone new to keto it can be very challenging to stick to a low-carb diet, even though fat is the cornerstone of this diet you should not be eating any and all kinds of fat. Healthy fats are essential, but what is healthy fat you might ask. Healthy fats would consist of grass-fed meats, (lamb, beef, goat, venison), wild caught fish and seafood, pastured pork & poultrys. Eggs and salt free butters can also be ingested. Be sure to stay away from starchy vegetables, fruit, and grains. Processed foods are in no way accepted in any shape or form on the ketogenic diet. Artificial sweeteners and milk can also pose a serious issue.

Reasons to Avoid Low Carb Diets

Low carb (carbohydrate), high protein diets are the latest dieting craze. However, before you jump on the band wagon, you may want to consider a few things:

1. Low carb (ketogenic) diets deplete the healthy glycogen (the storage form of glucose) stores in your muscles and liver. When you deplete glycogen stores, you also dehydrate, often causing the scale to drop significantly in the first week or two of the diet. This is usually interpreted as fat loss when it's actually mostly from dehydration and muscle loss. By the way, this is one of the reasons that low carb diets are so

popular at the moment – there is a quick initial but deceptive drop in scale weight.

Glycogenesis (formation of glycogen) occurs in the liver and muscles when adequate quantities of carbohydrates are consumed – very little of this happens on a low carb diet.

Glycogenolysis (breakdown of glycogen) occurs when glycogen is broken down to form glucose for use as fuel.

2. Depletion of muscle glycogen causes you to fatigue easily, and makes exercise and movement uncomfortable. Research indicates that muscle fatigue increases in almost direct proportion to the rate of depletion of muscle glycogen. Bottom line is that you don't feel energetic and you exercise and move less (often without realizing it) which is not good for caloric expenditure and basal metabolic rate (metabolism).

3. Depletion of muscle glycogen leads to muscle atrophy (loss of muscle). This happens because muscle glycogen (broken down to glucose) is the fuel of choice for the muscle during movement. There is always a fuel mix, but without muscle glycogen, the muscle fibers that contract, even at rest to maintain muscle tone, contract less when glycogen is not

immediately available in the muscle. Depletion of muscle glycogen also causes you to exercise and move less than normal which leads to muscle loss and the inability to maintain adequate muscle tone.

Also, in the absence of adequate carbohydrate for fuel, the body initially uses protein (muscle) and fat. The initial phase of muscle depletion is rapid, caused by the use of easily accessed muscle protein for direct metabolism or for conversion to glucose (gluconeogenesis) for fuel. Eating excess protein does not prevent this because there is a caloric deficit.

When insulin levels are chronically too low as they may be in very low carb diets, catabolism (breakdown) of muscle protein increases, and protein synthesis stops.

4. Loss of muscle causes a decrease in your basal metabolic rate (metabolism). Metabolism happens in the muscle. Less muscle and muscle tone means a slower metabolism which means fewer calories burned 24 hours-a-day.

5. Your muscles and skin lack tone and are saggy. Saggy muscles don't look good, cause saggy skin, and cause you to lose a healthy, vibrant look (even if you've also lost fat).

6. Some proponents of low carb diets recommend avoiding carbohydrates such as bread, pasta, potatoes, carrots, etc. because of they are high on the glycemic index, causing a sharp rise in insulin. Certain carbohydrates have always been, and will always be the bad guys: candy, cookies, baked goods with added sugar, sugared drinks, processed/refined white breads, pastas, and rice, and any foods with added sugar.

These are not good for health or weight loss.

However, carbohydrates such as fruits, vegetables, legumes, whole grain breads and pastas, and brown rice are good for health and weight loss. Just like with proteins and fats, these carbohydrates should be eaten in moderation. Large volumes of any proteins, fats or carbohydrates are not conducive to weight loss and health.

The effect of high glycemic foods is often exaggerated. It does matter, but to a smaller degree than is often portrayed. Also, the total glycemic effect of foods is influenced by the quantity of that food that you eat at a sitting. Smaller meals have a lower overall glycemic effect. Also, we usually eat several types of food at the same time, thereby reducing the average glycemic index of the meal, if higher glycemic foods are eaten.

Also, glycemic index values can be misleading because they are based on a standard 50 grams of carbohydrate consumed.

It wouldn't take much candy bar to get that, but it would take four cups of carrots. Do you usually eat four cups of carrots at a meal?

Regular exercisers and active people also are less effected by higher glycemic foods because much of the carbohydrate comsumed is immediately used to replenish glycogen stores in the liver and muscle.

By the way, if you're interested in lowering insulin levels, there is a great way to do that – exercise and activity.

7. Much of the weight loss on a low carb, high protein diet, especially in the first few weeks, is actually because of dehydration and muscle loss.

8. The percentage of people that re-gain the weight they've lost with most methods of weight loss is high, but it's even higher with low carb, high protein diets. This is primarily due to three factors:

> A. You have lost muscle. With that comes a slower metabolism which means fewer calories are burned 24 hours-a-day. A loss of muscle during the process of losing weight is

almost a guarantee for re-gaining the lost weight, and more.

B. You re-gain the healthy fluid lost because of glycogen depletion.

C. It's difficult to maintain that type of diet long-term.

D. You have not made a change to a long-term healthy lifestyle.

9. Eating too much fat is just not healthy. I know you've heard of people whose blood levels of cholesterol and triglycerides have decreased while on a low carb, high protein diet. This often happens with weight loss, but it doesn't continue when you're on a diet high in fat.

There are literally reams of research over decades that clearly indicates that an increase in consumption of animal products and/or saturated fat leads to increased incidences of heart disease, strokes, gallstones, kidney stones, arthritic symptoms, certain cancers, etc. For example, in comparing countries with varying levels of meat consumption, there is a direct relationship between the volume of meat consumption in a country and the incidence of digestive cancers (stomach, intestines, rectal, etc.).

Fat is certainly necessary, and desirable in your diet, but you should eat mostly healthy fats and in moderation.

Manufactured/synthetic "low fat" foods with lots of added sugar are not the answer. Neither are manufactured/synthetic "low carb" foods with artificial sweeteners or added fat. By the way, use of artificial sweeteners has never been shown to aid in weight loss and they may pose health problems.

10. As someone recently told me, "it must work, people are losing weight". People that are truly losing fat on low carb, high protein diets, are doing so because they are eating fewer calories – that's the bottom line. There is no magic – the same can be done on a healthy diet.

11. Low carb diets are lacking in fiber. Every plant-based food has some fiber. All animal products have no fiber. A lack of fiber increases your risk for cancers of the digestive tract (because transit time is lengthened) and cardiovascular disease (because of fiber's effect on fat and cholesterol). It also puts you at a higher risk for constipation and other bowel disorders.

12. Low carb diets lack sufficient quantities of the the many nutrients/phytonutrients/antioxidants found in

fruits, vegetables, legumes, and whole grains, necessary for health and aiding in the prevention of cancer and heart disease. In fact, you need these nutrients even more so when you're consuming too much fat as is often the case on a low carb, high protein diet.

13. Amercans already consume more than twice the amount of protein needed. Add to that a high protein diet and you have far too much protein consumption. By the way, most people don't realize that all fruits, all vegetables, all whole grains, and all legumes also contain protein. Animal products contain larger quantities of protein, but that may not be a good thing.

Excess dietary protein puts you at a higher risk for many health problems: gout (painful joints from high purine foods which are usually high protein foods), kidney disease, kidney stones, osteoporosis (excess dietary protein causes leeching of calcium from the bones). By the way, countries with lower, healthier intakes of protein also have a decreased incidence of osteoporosis.

14. Low carb, high protein diets cause an unhealthy physiological state called ketosis, a type of metabolic acidosis. You may have heard the phrase, "fat burns in the flame of carbohydrate". Excess acetyl CoA

cannot enter the Krebs Cycle (you remember the old Krebs Cycle) due to insufficient OAA. In other words, for fat to burn efficiently and without production of excess toxic ketones, sufficient carbohydrate must be available. Ketosis can lead to many health problems and can be very serious at it's extreme.

15. Bad breath. Often called "keto breath" or "acetone breath", it's caused by the production of acetones in a state of ketosis. So why the low carb, high protein craze? I believe there are several reasons.

> A. Weight loss (mostly muscle and muscle fluid) is often rapid during the first few weeks. This causes people to think they're losing fat rapidly.

> B. It gives you "permission" to eat the "bad foods": bacon, eggs, burgers, steak, cheese, etc. and lots of fat.

CHAPTER THREE

HOW TO AVOID COMMMON MISTAKES FOR BEGINNERS

Considering the variety of low carb diet variations out there, it can be hard to decide which one to stick to. For the most part, the low carb approach is perfect if you require to lose 30lbs or more. The most basic low carb diet that seems to work most effectively for individuals works as follows: for nine days you limit your carbohydrate intake to 30 grams everyday. On the 10th day, during the night time, you're allowed a high carbohydrate splurge, but you don't start consuming carbs until after 4pm. After this 10 day period your carb nights are spread out roughly once per week.

It sounds uncomplicated, doesn't it? If you've done any dieting in the past you've quite possibly tinkered around with diets similar to this. However, there are several common pitfalls that either impede progress or cause some people to make hardly any progress. I'll list a couple of them and give some remedies for how to prevent yourself from falling into these traps.

It is very effortless to ingest way too many carbs mainly because of the places you purchase meals. These days a lot of people don't cook and prepare their meals. Many individuals dine out, and although you have a "low carb salad" you will probably find yourself going over your limit by having food that has too many carbs without realizing it. A number of the low fat dressings have approximately 7-10g of carbs, and from time to time when you order a salad they will put greater than three portions. A good practice that my clients use is as simple as just getting the restaurant to put the dressing on the side and all you have to do is separate out a serving.

Going overboard on dairy is yet another frequent blunder. Unless you have a history of enduring dairy well, I strongly recommend most clients to refrain from it entirely when starting off. For most people, dairy can supercharge your urge for food which will cause you to consume too much.

Overeating is the next obvious pitfall. Unless you're eating a lot of whole foods and foods that have marginal processing, it may be easy to overeat. To guarantee your results, its best that you be wary of how much you consume. This is especially true if you're having difficulty experiencing fast enough results. Many of the processed "low carb" foods are very tasty which will either cause you to overeat that food, or just heighten your desire for food for the day which may lead to overeating.

Not receiving a good mix of fat and protein can lead to headaches or the dreaded "ketogenic flu" or keto flu. The signs are a bad throbbing headache and lots of fatigue. This develops as your body adjusts to not having enough carbs using fat instead. When your fat intake is lacking your body may have challenges getting sufficient energy. Don't be afraid of fat, just ensure to keep your saturated fat in check. Sources like avocados, olive oil and coconut oil are fantastic sources. Nuts are okay, you just have to look at the amount of carbs depending on the types of nuts or seeds you take in.

You may still have your steak and various fatty cuts of animal meat. Just make certain that fat sources vary. Coconut oil is a fat that consists of MCTs which your system is able to digest quickly to be used as energy. Other fats take longer to break down and by the time you get that keto flu headache, it can be far too late before symptoms are taken care of.

30 DAYS LOW CALORIES DIET PLAN

A 30 Day Diet Plan is most suitable for people that want to lose weight in a short period. There are several good diet plans available. A detox plan is a good example. A seven day detox meal plan is probably the best choice to lose the most weight in a week. It is a good way to cleanse the body of harmful toxins and lose weight at the same time.

Obviously the main concept of this plan is to consume very little calories. For this meal plan to be successful all of the calories must be counted before being consumed, and a person needs to figure out how many calories they should consume in a day to loose the amount of weight they want. This is calculated by height, weight, gender, age, and body mass index.

This meal plan falls under the category of detox diets. Although the name suggests that any amount of any kind of food can be eaten, in actuality only certain foods are allowed on certain days. The foods allowed to be consumed are vegetables, fruits, lean meat, and skim milk. It is important to drink a lot of water (8 glasses per day).

The Cabbage Soup Diet is another example of a diet plan. It is also considered to be a detox diet.

This meal plan consists of very little fat, all of the cabbage soup a person wants to eat, fruits, vegetables, and lean meat. Cabbage is a negative energy vegetable, this means the body burns more calories eating and digesting it than the cabbage contains. Therefore the more cabbage that is eaten the more weight a person will lose.

The recipe to make the cabbage soup is very simple:

1 small cabbage,

6 medium onions,

7 tomatoes,

2 green peppers.

Chop all the vegetables into small pieces, add water and boil until the vegetables are soft (about 20 minutes) then add salt and spices. On the first day of the diet people can eat all of the fruits except for bananas along with as much cabbage soup as they want.

Day 2. Soup and vegetables and a little bit of boiled potatoes are allowed. The vegetables can be fresh, boiled, or steamed.

Day 3 - Soup, fruit, and vegetables, but no potatoes.

Day 4 - A glass of fat free milk, 2 bananas, fruits, vegetables, and the cabbage soup.

Day 5 - 500 grams of boiled beef or skinless chicken or fish, soup, and tomatoes.

Day 6 - Green vegetables such as lettuce, meat, and of course cabbage soup.

Day 7 - Brown rice, vegetables, fruit juice (sugar free) and soup.

Repeat this for 31 days and you will see great changes.

BELOW SEE 10 HELPFUL HINTS.

1. Eat grains such as high fiber cereal, oatmeal, grits, etc. It is important to have a high fiber diet to keep the body cleansing regularly. Also, these carbohydrates start up your calorie burning machine. This is why fiber cereals are recommended for breakfast in most healthy eating plans.

2. Eat dark green leafy vegetables daily; such as; spinach, romaine lettuce, dark cabbage, kale and other greens. Dark vegetables are high in fiber and have many nutrients and vitamins that are needed for the body to function at a healthy level, and they are

low in calories. Because dark vegetables consist of a large percent of water you can indulge and still lose weight.

3. Eat at least 4 times each day, five when trying to lose weight. By eating often you won't have the opportunity to get hungry and overeat. Secondly, smaller meals are easier for the body to digest, burn off fat and unwanted calories. Because of how our bodies are designed, if you do not feed your body it will go into survival mode and hang onto extra weight versus releasing it.

4. Use portion control to lose weight. Never overeat. Put the appropriate portion of food on your plate. You have to know your portions, for example; steak or chicken should only be 4-5oz; most cooked carbs only 1/2 cup; fresh green vegetables, because they consist of a high percent of water, you can have 1 cup or more.

5. Read labels. They contain valuable information, such as: how many grams of sugar, sodium, carbs, calories, how much equals 1 serving, etc. Labels are your best friend. If you don't understand them it will be hard to lose weight.

6. Eat breakfast everyday. Breakfast is the most important meal of the day. When a healthy breakfast

is eaten it begins the calorie burning machine for the day. Whole grains and oatmeal are highly recommended because they get the metabolism working.

7. Eat fresh fruit but be selective on fruits eaten. Some fruits such as ripe bananas are extremely high in sugar and may be a detriment to your goals, but fruits like blueberries have antioxidants and help build your immune system and are low in calories.

8. Write down everything eaten in a journal. It is important to record everything that you eat. It allows you to see exactly what you are putting in your mouth all day long. It gives you better insight on why you may not be losing weight. You must record everything that you eat, what time and how much eaten.

9. Don't snack while watching TV. When you eat in front of the TV there may be very little connection on how much your mouth is taking in. This leads to overeating.

10. Don't eat empty calories. If you want to lose weight, make every calorie count. Some foods have great value, while others taste good but have no nutritional value and lots of calories. Know the difference

Balanced Three-Meal Two-Snack Plan

This meal plan is based on splitting daily calorie intake in three meals and two snacks. Mainly, lots of lean protein and veggies are loaded in this diet program.

Breakfast: For starting the day, half cup of egg whites, 1 apple, whole wheat toast and a tablespoon of butter or 2 tablespoons of peanut butter is enough.

Snack: For midday munching, 8 oz. of zero fat Greek yogurt, half cup of berries, 1 tablespoon of agave nectar or a protein bar (200 calories) are considered best.

Lunch: Lunch can include salad made with 3 cups spinach, 2 tablespoons full fat dressing and 4 oz. grilled chicken, along with a half cup garbanzo beans.

Dinner: For ending the day well, you can go for a baked salmon, half sweet potato, and 4 cups roasted vegetables cooked in 2 tablespoons olive oil.

The Vegan Plan

It is one of the latest diet plans, which is mainly popularized by a good number of celebrities. This diet program mainly involves cutting down the intake of processed foods to lose more weight. This plan does not obligate the dieters to stay hungry by cutting down the consumption. It simply replaces the processed food items with healthy ones.

Breakfast: One cup tofu (scrambled), two whole wheat bread slices, two wedges raw cantaloupe and one tablespoon of vegan margarine spread can start the day well.

Snack: One table spoon flax seed in 4 oz. vanilla soy yogurt can serve the purpose.

Lunch: A perfect midday meal includes black bean and sweet potato salad with 2 oz. tofu for a protein kick.

Dinner: One cup quinoa (well cooked) and a single serving of grilled vegetables is suitable for ending the day well.

So, these are some simple and effective 30 day meal plans for getting back in shape easily.

CHAPTER FOUR

30 DAY MEAL PREP TO GET IN SHAPE

The most effective way is typically to continually get back to the fundamentals as well as making use of what works. Stick to good information and you should not follow the newest diets or even fads on losing weight and you're going to be fine. Now we will look into how nutrition along with what you take in may help you lose a substantial amount of unwanted weight.

What to eat

Water rich food items

Try eating plenty of water rich foods which includes vegetables along with fruit. Water rich foods are not just beneficial, they can be a very important factor in shedding weight. Any of these water rich foods are actually very much less dense and don't deliver a great deal of calories but while doing so continue to keep us feeling satisfied. Water will also help to flush out impurities which happen to be one of several vehicles that stick in to additional fat in our body. The easiest way to make this happen should be to have a side salad with each and every meal that you have and additionally switch out snacks such as sugars to fruit.

Antioxidants and vitamin rich foods

Foods containing more antioxidants would be a requirement to include in your diet plan should you want to lose weight. Nearly all food items that are rich in antioxidants are great for slimming down as they are lower in calories. Vitamins also help our bodies perform better. With the body staying at a proper level, it is usually far easier to get rid of fat since the body stream is much smoother and takes away harmful toxins easier.

Things to refrain from

Unhealthy fats

What's as vital as picking the right foods is understanding what to steer clear of. This is an obvious one: refrain from fatty foods. This is really important simply because fatty foods don't just store as fat on your body but it makes you truly feel exhausted. Any time you feel really worn out you will find a higher chance you don't want to exercise as well. Unhealthy fats also block your system and therefore can make it more difficult for your body to cleanse and remove toxic compounds. These kinds of toxins keep hold of body fat and increases excess fat.

Sugar

Remember to keep far away from foods that have sugar. This includes candy, junk food, instant foods and more. Sugar is known as a supply of instant energy. The negative thing is if not burnt off, sugars can become extra fat and store in your body. Sugar is also high in calories and also low in nutrition. It is that which we call "empty calories". Foods which happen to be dense but are without any nutrients. Make sure you stick with purely natural sugars like fresh fruits rather than refined sugars which can do no good.

Since you now know exactly what to consume and just what not to consume, possibly the best way to lose more weight is generally to manage the portion you take in. Avoid overeating and you are on the right course. Even though it could be tough from time to time, the simplest way to accomplish this is to drink a big glass of water before you start to eat. This way, the body feels a bit more satiated just before you eat and it also helps clean out any toxic compounds which in turn helps to get rid of fat at the same time. A different way will be to save half your meal and eat it later. Eating a smaller amount but more often can help boost metabolism and this results in fat burning.

If you keep to the information above, you're going to be on the right track to creating your best physique. Reducing your weight isn't a difficult task and should not be overwhelming. Many weight loss trends help you to slim down but they do not keep us healthy and in most cases the excess weight returns. Maintaining everything we have discussed, it will be better to keep the body weight away once you get going and also stay in an improved condition. Therefore, begin your journey now and please remember the principles of a healthier lifestyle.

Would you believe it if someone told you that eating certain foods could help you lose unwanted pounds? Naturally you wouldn't, but it is true that certain foods can help in reducing your weight. Imagine losing weight simply because you eat more of these particular foods. Without a doubt, all these fat burning foods should be included in your diet. If you eat these foods three times a day, and remain active; you will be amazed at the results.

1. Beans: These contain a ton of protein, carbs, and fiber. They give you the fuel that your body needs to work, not feel hungry, and ensure that your body is working like it should. As a result, it's important to add beans to your dietary plan.

2. Cinnamon: Research indicates that consuming as little as a quarter tablespoon of cinnamon will maintain healthy blood sugar levels and increase insulin production. You'll have more energy while craving less sweets. In the end you won't be burdened with extra pounds.

3. Fish: Fish reduces leptin, a fatty acid which is needed. Leptin will offset obesity and the slowing down of your metabolism. Also, eating fish increases levels of omega-3 acids, which can be instrumental in keeping your heart in good shape. Therefore, fish is great to include in your diet as a way to stay healthy and lose weight.

4. Berries and Apples: Certain fruits such as berries and apples contain the water-binding ingredient pectin. Eating fruits that contain a lot of pectin inhibits the absorption of fat and cholesterol. Therefore keeping unwanted fat away will be a lot easier.

5. Garlic may smell funny but it's a star in boosting metabolism and aiding weight loss.

6. Ginger: Ginger is a vasodilator, meaning that it expands the body's blood vessels. This raises the body's metabolic level, aiding in weight loss.

7. Soybeans: These beans can be a fantastic way to consume protein that is low in fat. Amazingly, it maintains a low glycemic index and a stable sugar level, so you can eat sweet foods with no effects.

8. Green tea: Great tea is better for you than coffee. It can increase your metabolism from 28% to 77% while at the same time refreshing you. The greater amount you consume, the more of an effect you will observe in the rate of your metabolism.

Lose 20 lbs In Two Weeks

In 1995, WHO (World Health Organisation) estimated that 200 million adults and 18 million children under 5 years of age are obese. In 2000, it reported that this figure has increased to more than 300 million. Hectic lifestyles is the most blamed factor. Overweight people are much prone to heart diseases, high blood pressure, cholesterol levels, hypertension, cancer, arthritis, sleep apnea, strokes, brain damage and diabetes. Apart from this, obese people also develop low self-esteem and have appearance issues. They are looked upon as unhappy, unhealthy, tired, sick or lazy individuals. Losing weight increases self-esteem, induces the feel good factor and enhances the appearance, besides preventing major diseases.

Therefore weight loss and fitness are issues of growing concern. People worldwide crave to shed their extra pounds and stay fit. Here we share with you some knowledge on how to lose 20 lbs in just two weeks. Of course, it takes a little bit effort on your part.

Dieting and exercising

Plan your diet. Say a big no to junk foods and carbonated drinks. Avoid all calorie rich foods. Calculate your calorie intake, and restrict it to a certain level depending upon your energy requirements. Each and every single calorie counts when you are dieting.

Increase your metabolic rate, which is the rate at which your body processes and uses the food you eat. It is an easy and sensible technique to lose weight. Try taking several small meals a day instead of taking it in large amounts a few times a day. This burns your fats faster. Constant eating helps develop a higher metabolism within you in order to accommodate your frequent eating, hence burning calories fast.

Increase your physical activities, stay active, and include fibre rich diets to increase your metabolic rate. Including green tea in your daily fluid intake also helps in increasing your metabolism and energy level.

Go in for a detoxification of your system. It removes all the potentially harmful and toxic substances from your system and cleanses it. Follow a detox diet. Juice based detox diets are good options, especially, the lemonade diet. Detoxification helps you drop your liquid weight in a little time. Maintain a healthy lifestyle after detoxification.

Take eight glasses of water daily. Water plays an important role in weight loss by speeding up your metabolism and by ensuring proper digestion, besides rehydrating your body. Staying hydrated makes you feel more energetic, thus boosting your metabolic rate. Drinking water also reduces your strong craving for food.

Also, be sure to maintain your body's nutrition while dieting. Consume nutritious but low calorie food stuff. It is recommended that you cut 150-300 calories from your daily diet, and burn 150-300 calories in exercising. Scientific studies say, dieting is the best method for weight loss. But in order to achieve effective weight loss, doing a combo of dieting and exercising is necessary.

You will have to spend an hour or more to achieve your desired goal of losing 20 lbs in 2 weeks. Exercising should be intensive and vigorous, instead of merely walking. Doing the same kind of work outs render it boring. To ensure that it is interesting, do a variety of activities like jogging, cycling, weight lifting, hiking, rowing, etc. Doing some abdominal crunches keeps in check the belly contours. Exercises, besides giving your desired weight loss, also ensure that you are in a good shape. It does more good too.

Have the right mind set

To get motivated and to stay motivated are two important facets of your mind settings that will help you in reaching your predetermined goal of getting rid of those 20 lbs.

"Many of life's failures are people who did not realize how close they were to success when they gave up" - Thomas Edison.

Motivation and perseverance are essentials that keep you in the right mind set to help you attain your dream come true body weight. Motivation is the conscious or subconscious driving force, which when combines with steady persistence makes you achieve your goal. It contributes to your thoughts and actions.

Reason away: Why do you want to lose weight? Is it to look better? To feel more confident? To walk that ramp? To get that attention from your crush? Or anything else? You state it. Reasoning helps you take the necessary action by fixing your attitude.

Here are some points that will help you stay motivated:

· Make up your mind that you will never quit.

· Stay focussed on the end result.

· Keep track of your successes.

· Keep your motivation on high levels.

The thing next in getting the right mind set is positive thinking. There is a dramatic power in positive thinking. Positive thinking is a mental attitude that anticipates and admits conducive conditions in all the spheres of life in terms of growth, expansion and success. It is expressed through one's words and actions.

CHAPTER FIVE

THE PRONS AND CONS OF LOW CARB DIET

Low carb diets are all the rage. They seem to work for many people, and these people swear by them. Unfortunately, they don't work for everyone who tries them. These people end up using an alternative method of weight loss. A low carbohydrate diet is basically cutting back or eliminating any foods which contain starches and carbohydrates and instead eating foods high in protein. For those who are curious about a low carb diet, you need to make sure it's right for you, your current health status, personal habits and lifestyle, and your ultimate goals.

With trying anything new, there are pros and cons to consider. And when it comes to dieting, you must be aware of all the issues related to your weight-loss and any weight-loss diet. The following gives you the "skinny" on the pros and cons in regards to low carbohydrate diets:

Pro - Because a low carbohydrate diet is all about eliminating carbs and not actual food, you can usually eat to your heart's content.

Con - Because you have to restrict yourself to certain foods, it can get monotonous.

Pro - Since low carb diets are so popular, you can find information about them quickly and easily.

Con - There is so much information about low carb diets it can get confusing and you still may not know everything you need to know before starting a low carb diet.

Pro - By eliminating foods high in carbs, you lose weight more quickly.

Con - When you eliminate certain food types, you also eliminate certain nutrients your body needs for optimal health.

Pro - It's easy to follow a low carb diet, the variety of foods can keep you satisfied.

Con - The foods you need to eat on a low carbohydrate diet can get expensive.

Pro - Low carb diets will get your cravings under control.

Con - You will go through withdrawals eating no or low carb foods only.

Pro - You will see faster weight loss when you eat low to no carbohydrate foods all the time.

Con - Low carb diets are harder to follow during special events, holidays and occasions when there are only high carb foods available.

Pro - Low carb diet are very effective for weight loss.

Con - To succeed on a low carbohydrate diet, you must have strong willpower.

Pro - Your immune system will improve with a low carbohydrate diet.

Con - Too many saturated fats are bad for the health of your heart.

Pro - You learn to eat healthier by ridding your body of carbs.

Con - Some carbs are not bad – complex carbs have nutritional value.

Pro - You will get high amounts of protein and can still enjoy eating the meats you love.

Con - People who are vegetarian will have trouble getting all the nutrition they need since they don't eat meat.

THE BASIC PRINCIPLE OF KETOGENIC DIET

One very popular weight loss program that many people are trying out are low carb diets. But, are low carb diets really that effective?

To an extent, yes, low carb diets can make dieting a great deal easier. Typically people using a low carb approach tend to have less hunger issues to deal with, tend to see reduced bloating, hence they look thinner, and also tend to enjoy the food since you're allowed to have more dietary fat with these approaches.

But, that said, there are some important things you must realize before starting up on a low carb diet. If you don't recognize these factors, you could wind up getting into quite a bit of trouble on a low carb diet and not see the types of results you're looking for.

Here's what you need to know about low carb diets.

Low Carb Diets And Exercise Carbs

First, it's going to be very important that you are having carb ups at some point during your exercise workout. This can be before or after the workout is finished, or in the form of one very large carb-up on the weekend. Doing so will help to ensure that the body has enough muscle glycogen storage to be able to continue on with the exercise programs you are asking it to perform.

Neglecting to take in carbs at this point can lead to feelings of fatigue, and may even cause you to stop your fat loss workouts altogether.

Low Carb Diets Shouldn't Limit Vegetables

Next, you also want to be sure you're not limiting vegetables at all while on a low carb diet. Doing so would be very problematic because these are filled with plenty of vitamins, minerals, and antioxidants. Not too mention they are low in calories, high in fiber, and are one of the best diet foods to be eating.

So, don't limit your vegetable consumption even if you are on a low carb diet. You will want to watch out for the varieties that do contain more starch, such as peas, corn, and carrots, but otherwise you can eat quite a few without worry.

Low Carb Diets and Water Intake

Finally, the last thing to keep in mind is that low carb diets do tend to have a dehydrating effect on the body, therefore it's going to be very important that you make sure you're drinking plenty of liquids.

It would be a smart move to bump up your water intake slightly from what you'd normally drink – about 10-12 cups of fluid altogether should be plenty.

So, be sure you're keeping these points in mind when considering a low carb approach. While some people just do not feel well at all on low-carb diets, many others do have good success on them.

CHAPTER SIX

WHAT IS THE KETO DIET?

The keto diet involves going long spells on extremely low (no higher than 30g per day) to almost zero g per day of carbs and increasing your fats to a really high level (to the point where they may make up as much as 65% of your daily macronutrients intake.) The idea behind this is to get your body into a state of ketosis. In this state of ketosis the body is supposed to be more inclined to use fat for energy, and research says it does just this. Depleting your carbohydrate/ glycogen liver stores and then moving onto fat for fuel means you should end up shredded.

You then follow this basic platform from say Monday until Sat 12pm (afternoon) (or Sat 7pm, depending on whose version you read). Then from this time until 12 midnight Sunday night (so up to 36 hours later) you carb up.

(Some say, and this will also be dictated by your body type, that you can go nuts in the carb up and eat anything you want and then there are those that more wisely – in my view – prescribe still sticking to the clean carbs even during your carb up.)

So calculating your numbers is as simple as the following...

Calculate your required maintenance level of daily calories...

(if you are looking to drop quickly use 1300. I would not advise this, if you want a more level drop in body fat use 1500 and if you are going to actually attempt to maintain or possibly put on some lean muscle mass then use 1700)

Body weight in pounds x 15= a

Protein for the day 1g per body weight in pounds= b

Bx4=c (c= number of calories allotted to your daily protein allowance).

a-c= d (d= amount of calories to be allotted to fat intake).

D/9= g per day of fat to be consumed.

The end calculation should leave you with a very high number for your fat intake.

Now for those of you wondering about energy levels: Especially for training because there are no carbs, with there being such a high amount of fat in the diet you feel quite full and the fat is a very good fuel source for your body. One adaptation that I have made is to actually have a nice fish fillet about an hour before I train and I find it gives me enough energy to get through my workout. (I am aware of the arguments made to not have fats 2-3 hours either side of training. While I won't have fats 2-3 hours after training as I want quick absorption and blood flow, I see no issue with slowing everything down before training so my body has access to a slow digesting energy source).

There are some that say to have a 30g carb intake immediately after training – just enough to fill liver glycogen levels. And then there are those that say having even as much as that may push you out of ketosis, the state you are trying to maintain.

During my carb up period, for the sake of those who would like to know if you can get in shape and still eat the things you want (in moderation), for the first six weeks I will be relaxed about what I eat in this period but then the following 6 weeks I will only eat clean carbs.

I also like to make sure that the first workout of the week – as in a Monday morning workout – is a nice long full hour of work so I start cutting into the liver glycogen immediately.

KETOGENIC DIETS AND WEIGHT LOSS AND BODYBUILDING

A ketogenic diet is one where there are no carbs. Without carbohydrates the body burns fat as the primary fuel source. Since this is happening the body can tap into stored bodyfat for energy and we can end up leaner. While that is possible we need to look at what may happen.

For starters your energy will be drained. Without carbohydrates your body won't know what energy source to turn to for a few days so you may experience feelings of weakness while you train or until your body becomes adapted to using fat. While this isn't a bad thing you must understand that you have to change your training intensity. There's no way that you can keep training at a high intensity while you use one of these diets.

The next thing that you have to understand about using a ketogenic diet for weight loss or bodybuilding is that you need to eat more protein then normal. Since you don't have carbs, and carbs are protein sparing, you need to consume more protein so you don't lose muscle tissue. So make sure that you are eating at least six meals per day with a serving of protein coming every meal.

Then you have to make sure that you are getting enough fiber. Look to consume fiber from various sources such as green vegetables and fiber powder or pills like physillum husk. Now you need to add some healthily nutritional supplements since you want to make sure that you do your best to burn fat on these keto diets for weight loss and bodybuilding. First, make sure you consume healthy fats like omega-3 fish oils, cla, and gla. These fats will help to burn more body fat. Then you want to purchase a good branch chain amino acid powder as bcaas help to retain muscle mass and prevent muscle breakdown.

KETOGENIC DIETS FOR MANAGING TYPE 2 DIABETES

Ketogenic diets have been in use since 1924 in pediatrics as a treatment for epilepsy. A ketogenic (keto) diet is one that is high in fat and low in carbs. The design of the ketogenic diet is to shifts the body's metabolic fuel from burning carbohydrates to fats. With the keto diet, the body metabolizes fat, instead of sugar, into energy. Ketones are a byproduct of that process.

Over the years, ketogenic diets have been used to treat diabetes. One justification was that it treats diabetes at its root cause by lowering carbohydrate intake leading to lower blood sugar, which in turn, lowers the need for insulin which minimizes insulin resistance and associated metabolic syndrome. In this way, a ketogenic diet may improve blood glucose (sugar) levels while at the same time reducing the need for insulin. This point of view presents keto diets as a much safer and more effective plan than injecting insulin to counteract the consumption of high carbohydrate foods.

A keto diet is actually a very restrictive diet. In the classic keto diet for example, one gets about 80 percent of caloric requirements from fat and 20 percent from proteins and carbohydrates. This is a marked departure from the norm where the body runs on energy from sugar derived from carbohydrate digestion but by severely limiting carbohydrates, the body is forced to use fat instead.

A ketogenic diet requires healthy food intake from beneficial fats, such as coconut oil, grass-pastured butter, organic pastured eggs, avocado, fish such as salmon, cottage cheese, avocado, almond butter and raw nuts (raw pecans and macadamia). People on ketogenic diets avoid all bread, rice, potatoes, pasta, flour, starchy vegetables, and most dairy. The diet is low in vitamins, minerals, and nutrients and requires supplementation.

A low carbohydrate diet is frequently recommended for people with type 2 diabetes because carbohydrates turn to blood sugar which in large quantities cause blood sugar to spike. Thus, for a diabetic who already has high blood sugar, eating additional sugar-producing foods is like courting danger. By switching the focus from sugar to fat, some patients can experience reduced blood sugar.

Changing the body's primary energy source from carbohydrates to fat leaves behind the byproduct of fat metabolism, ketones in the blood. For some diabetic patients, this can be dangerous as a buildup of ketones may create a risk for developing diabetic ketoacidosis (DKA). DKA is a medical emergency requiring immediate medical attention. DKA signs include consistently high blood sugar, dry mouth, polyuria, nausea, breath that has a fruit-like odor and breathing difficulties. Complications can lead to a diabetic coma.

For many people, the ketogenic diet is a great option for weight loss. It is very different and allows the person on the diet to eat a diet that consists of foods that you may not expect.

When you eat a very low amount of carbs your body gets put into a state of ketosis. What this means is your body burns fat for energy. How low of an amount of carbs do you need to eat in order to get into ketosis? Well, it varies from person to person, but it is a safe bet to stay under 25g net carbs. Many would suggest that when you are in the "induction phase" which is when you are actually putting your body into ketosis, you should stay under 10g net carbs.

If you aren't sure what net carbs are, let me help you. Net carbs are the amount of carbs you eat minus the amount of dietary fiber. So if on the day you eat a total of 35g of net carbs and 13g of dietary fiber, your net carbs for the day would be 22. Simple enough, right?

So besides weight loss what else is good about keto? Well, many people talk about their improved mental clarity when on the diet. Another benefit is having an increase in energy. Yet another is a decreased appetite.

One thing to worry about when going on the ketogenic diet is something called "keto flu." Not everyone experiences this, but for those that do it can be tough. You will feel lethargic and you may have a headache. It won't last very long. When you feel this way make sure you get plenty of water and rest to get through it.

If this sounds like the kind of diet you would be interested in, then what are you waiting for? Dive head first into keto. You won't believe the results you get in such a short amount of time.

CHAPTER SEVEN

HOW TO ENSURE YOUR VEGAN MEALS AND RECIPES ARE LOW-CALORIE

Vegan Weight Loss Advice

Certain folk have trouble losing weight on the vegan lifestyle. Although the majority will experience weight loss on the vegan diet, there are always some who wonder what they are doing wrong. There are simple and easy measures that you can take to ensure that all of your vegan meals and recipes that you prepare are complementing your weight loss efforts.

1. Go steady with the oil

Olive oil and other healthy oils are essential for optimal health and will help keep your hair, skin and nails beautiful. However, because olive oil is a form of fat (the healthy type), it is very high in energy content. Therefore, to keep your vegan meals low-calorie you should measure out your olive oil with a spoon just as your recipes call for, rather than simply pouring the oil into your dish.

2. Keep an eye on your nut portions

Many vegan recipes feature walnuts, brazil nuts or other gourmet nuts to make the meal flavoursome and satisfying. If you are hoping to see some weight loss, however, only add nuts to one of your meals per day – not all three! This will help keep your diet low-calorie and low-fat and will ultimately result in a slimmer physique.

3. Don't eat too much vegan junk-food

You should endeavour to make your own wholesome vegan meals and recipes as often as you are able, rather than opting for quick vegan junk food. This will make you in control of your food, and you can make your vegan meals and recipes as low-calorie and low-fat as you please. Vegan junk food on the other hand is terrible for weight loss, with packet chips, cookies, chocolates, salty nuts and soft-drinks the main offenders. These foods are too high in energy to eat on a regular basis, so please stick to making your own fresh vegan meals to guarantee weight loss.

4. Share your vegan baking with your friends

There are so many beautiful and tasty vegan sweets and dessert recipes that you can make nowadays, and let's be fair, every vegan should enjoy their fair share. But when you do bake, only make one serving of the recipe rather than doubling or tripling it. Also, share your recipes with friends, family and colleagues to show a giving spirit and mostly to save yourself from unnecessary emotional eating.

You can take control of your calorie intake on the vegan diet to ensure a steady weight loss. Remember to go steady with the olive oil, keep an eye on you nut portions, limit your vegan junk-food and share your baking with friends. Making wise choices as such will help make your weight loss a sure success on the vegan diet.

VEGAN MEAL PLAN

Switching to a vegan diet can be a great way to lose weight and get healthier. A vegan does not eat any foods that contain or are made with animal products of any kind. This can be a restrictive lifestyle, but many people choose to make this change and it is no surprise with all the weight that can be lost. No matter if it is due to religious reasons, health reasons, or concern for animal welfare, a vegan diet can really change how you feel and how you look.

If you are thinking about making the move to a vegan lifestyle it might help for you to have a vegan meal plan. There are so many delicious options for vegan foods. This meal plan is just a jumping off point. It is a great idea to buy some vegan cookbooks. It is also great to check out the thousands of vegan recipes that are online. Be adventurous and try new things. Here are some vegan recipes for breakfast, lunch, dinner, and dessert.

Breakfast

• Scrambled Tofu

• 1 ½ tablespoon safflower oil

• 3 tablespoons diced onion

• 1 diced Serrano chili

• 1/2 teaspoon ground cumin

• 3 tablespoons chopped cilantro

• 20 oz tofu

• Salsa of your choosing

Instructions

Heat the oil; add in onion and sauté for 1 to 2 minutes. Add the chilies and cumin, cook for a few minutes. Crumble the tofu and cook, stirring frequently. Mix in the cilantro and season with salt. Serve with warm tortillas and salsa.

Lunch

- Sweet Corn Soup

- 6 ears of corn

- 1 tablespoon corn oil

- 1 small onion

- 1/2 cup grated celery root

- 7 cups water or vegetable stock

- Salt to taste

1.   Shuck the corn and slice off the kernels.

2.   In a large soup pot put in the oil, onion, celery root, and one cup of water. Let that mixture stew under low heat until the onion is soft.

3.   Add the corn, salt and remaining water and bring it to a boil.

4.   Cool briefly and then puree in a blender, then wait for it to cool before putting it through a food mill.

5.   Reheat and add salt and pepper to taste.

Dinner

Seared Portobello Mushrooms

• 1 large Portobello mushroom, stem removed

• Olive oil as needed

• Salt and pepper

• Shallot vinaigrette

1.   Slice the mushroom into wide slices.

2.   Brush both sides with oil and set them in the skillet over high heat. Sear for 4 to 5 minutes.

3.   Once they start to brown remove them and place them on a platter with salt and pepper to taste.

4.   Add vinaigrette to the top for flavor.

Lentil and Onion Croquettes

• 2 cups chopped yellow onion

- 2 tablespoons olive oil

- 1/2 cup finely chopped carrot

- 2 cups bread crumbs

- 1 cup lentils

- 3/4 cup celery chopped

- Salt and pepper

1.   In a skillet over low heat cook the onion in the olive oil.

2.   In a saucepan combine the lentils, celery, carrots, and salt covered with water. Bring this to a boil and then lower the heat to a simmer for about 30 minutes.

3.   Drain the liquid. Puree the lentils until smooth.

4.   Mix the lentils with the onion and bread crumbs. Season with salt and pepper.

5.   Allow the mixture to cool and then form it into 3 inch rounds. Fry the croquette balls in olive oil and set them on a paper towel to soak up the excess oil.

Dessert

Strawberry Ice

- 1 quart ripe strawberries

- Stevia (to taste)

1. Pull out the core of the berries.

2. Puree them in a food processor.

3. Put stevia into a saucepan. Add half a cup of the puree into the stevia and heat stirring constantly until it is all dissolved.

4. Add in the puree and freeze.

CHAPTER EIGHT

STAYING HEALTHY WITH VEGAN MEALS ON A KETO DIET

There are many reasons why people should be careful with what they eat. First off, they have too many activities to attend to every day. With each activity, their body consumes and burn energy. The environment is also no longer as safe as it was. Even the air that supplies the oxygen contains particles and bacteria that could cause diseases. One way to protect their body from diseases is by eating healthy and nutritious food.

Nowadays, people try to keep their bodies protected and healthy through exercise and healthy diets. Many people follow a vegetarian diet plan. However, even with this plan, people may still be at risk of some illnesses.

When a person prepares a meal, he has to remember that every ingredient he uses is special and is meant for something. Some ingredients are used to give the meal a pleasing taste. But, most ingredients are used to infuse it with nutrients and vitamins that the body needs.

Meat, for example, is a good source of protein. Proteins act as the building blocks of the body. They are needed to develop the muscles, cartilages, and bones. Even skin and blood needs them. Without them, you may stay in the gym the whole day and obtain very little result. Going for high protein, low carb vegetarian foods is actually going to help you have stronger muscles and a leaner body.

Carbohydrate is another component that the human body needs. It is what keeps people doing what they have to do by helping them obtain energy. Unfortunately, having too much of it could lead to serious and long-term diseases like diabetes and high blood pressure. In fact, dieticians and other health experts recommend some low carb vegetarian recipes to people suffering from such conditions.

People who try to indulge in vegetarian meals without understanding how it works may deny their body some nutrients. That is because this diet may not include the sources of proteins, carbohydrates and some vitamins that are required by the body.

On the other hand, following a vegan meal may actually be a good start to a healthier lifestyle. But, a person who intends to shift to this kind of diet should first look at what he needs. He must consider his activities and health conditions. He needs to determine what he actually wants to develop or remove from his body. Taking these things into consideration would help him obtain faster results, and a fitter and healthier body. Most importantly, it would help him determine what vegetarian diet plan to follow.

On the vegan diet you should experience a profound detoxification of your body, a restoral of your health, a newfound zest for life, and of course, weight loss. Most folk who go on the vegan diet will lose weight, but there are the minority who do not. What are they doing wrong? Let's look at several mistakes that they may be making which are greatly sabotaging their weight loss efforts.

1. Over-eating

All foods should be eaten in moderation – regardless of how healthy they are. For example, one single banana is low in calories (approximately 100). Most vegans love bananas and will happily consume two or three a day. But what if you had 10 bananas in one day plus your other meals? This means that you will be consuming 1000 calories per day with bananas alone. This may sound like a crazy example, but I'm sure it gets the point across. You should eat all foods in moderation. Eat generous sized meals but don't make yourself sick. Eat your meals with intuition, balance and self-control. This will ensure that you will lose weight on the vegan diet.

2. Too many Nuts

Nuts are an essential food for those on the vegan diet due to their high nutritional properties, particularly for their protein and healthy-fat content. But the problem is when you have too many as the calories add up fast. Many folk say that they can easily polish off an entire container of nuts in one sitting. I'm sorry to say this, but if you intend to lose weight on the vegan diet, you need to limit your serving of nuts. Don't deprive yourself of them, but one or two handfuls per day should be sufficient.

3. Too much oil

Olive oil and other healthy oils are very good for your hair, skin and nails and you should consume a couple of tablespoons every day. But these oils are also very high in calorie content so please measure out your servings with a spoon, rather than happily pour the oil into your dish like a free-spirited chef. Just remember, by sensibly measuring out your olive oil you can keep your vegan meals low-calorie and low-fat. This will in turn help you to lose weight.

4. Too many avocadoes

Avocadoes are considered one of the top superfoods in the world. Due to their super-high nutrient content, they can help boost your health and make you beautiful on the inside and outside. But they are also high in energy due to their healthy fat content, so please stick to half to one medium sized avocado per day. Limiting your avocado portions will help ensure that your vegan meals will be low-fat and low-calorie.

5. Vegan Junk-Food

Nobody should eat much junk food, whether vegan or not. The vegan junk food list is long, with the common rogues being packet chips, biscuits, chocolate, lollies and soft-drinks. So stay away from these foods most of the time and only have these on special occasions. It's all about eating in moderation. Eat this food only a couple of times per week rather than on a daily basis.

These are the most common causes why some vegans cannot lose weight. Really, the key is to enjoy your vegan food in moderation, limit your portion of nuts, oils and avocadoes, and steer away from vegan junk food.

Benefits of a Vegan Lifestyle

One common notion about becoming a vegan is that you'll miss foods that are not part of the diet, such as meat. However, most people who begin following a plant-based diet come to find it expansive and empowering instead of restrictive. The truth is you will eat better than you did in the past and feel better as well. Cravings for meat, fish, and dairy products will dissipate over time until they are not missed. If you are thinking about becoming a vegan, below are six benefits of the lifestyle that may help your decision.

Deeper Compassion

A vegan's compassion extends its reach to all living creatures. With increased compassion comes greater acceptance of all life and the appreciation that it adds value to our own, making us stronger.

Expanded Palate

Vegans learn to enjoy a very wide range of vegetables which leads to an expanded palate. Recipes abound for cooking every vegetable imaginable. When veggies are just a side dish, it's convenient to settle for a few of them to complement meat, such as potato salad, peas and carrots, or corn. Once veggies are the main dish, however, one starts to appreciate many more ingredients enriching the dining experience.

Global Impact

The vegan lifestyle is much more than food. It's about the environment, climate, sustainable development, efficient allocation of food sources, and animal welfare. Many of the themes associated with going green are linked to veganism. When one chooses to be a vegan, one participates and supports these themes. The impact of eating vegan is so powerful, that if everyone did it constantly or even occasionally, many of these issues would resolve themselves.

Increased Mobility

Nutritionists, dietitians, and health scientists are confirming the health benefits of a plant-based diet over a meat-based one. Lower blood pressure, reduced risk of heart disease and cancer, and longer life spans are possible outcomes of a vegan diet. Fewer health problems mean that one is more active and mobile and can enjoy life more fully.

Larger Social Network

The vegan community is large and growing. Vegans enjoy sharing their experiences and finding companions who understand the reasons for their eating habits. Meeting and connecting with new people is one of the fun social aspects of being vegan.

New Knowledge

The vegan diet is focused on ingredients, health, and nutrition. To enjoy vegan food and stay healthy, one inevitably learns more about nutrition and the impact of ingredients on health. Over time, by paying attention to what it consumed and the value of each ingredient, one becomes familiar with vitamins, minerals, protein, fiber, antioxidants, and phytonutrients and with it comes new knowledge and power.

The benefits of a vegan lifestyle make one a more empowered person. New experiences lead to new ideas and new ways to enjoy and fully appreciate life. Try eating more vegan meals and enjoy the positive impact.

CHAPTER NINE

HOW TO FOLLOW A PLANT-BASED KETOGENIC DIET

So how exactly do you slip into ketosis without loading up on butter and bacon? And how can you ensure that your nutrient needs are still being met while following a plant-based ketogenic diet?

The key is to swap out your starchy veggies for low-carb alternatives while also filling your diet with plenty of plant-based fats and proteins. This can help you stay under your carbohydrate goal and provide your body with the important vitamins and minerals that it needs to stay healthy.

High-carb foods that should be limited in your diet include:

• High-Sugar Fruits (apples, oranges, bananas, grapes, etc.)

• Starchy vegetables (potatoes, sweet potatoes, winter squash, peas, corn, etc.)

- Sugar (including honey, maple syrup, agave syrup, etc.)

- Legumes (beans, lentils, peas, etc.)

- Grains (wheat products, rice, quinoa, cereal, etc.)

Instead, be sure to include plenty of nutrient-rich, low-carb plant-based foods in your diet, such as:

- Fermented foods (tempeh, natto, etc.)

- Leafy greens (kale, chard, spinach, collard greens, etc.)

- Non-starchy vegetables (asparagus, carrots, cauliflower, onions, mushrooms, peppers, etc.)

- Nuts (almonds, walnuts, pistachios, pecans, etc.)

- Seeds (chia seeds, flax seeds, hemp seeds, pumpkin seeds, etc.)

- Low-sugar fruits (blackberries, raspberries, strawberries, etc.)

- Healthy fats (coconut oil, MCT oil, olive oil)

Including enough protein in your diet can be challenging on any plant-based diet, let alone a plant-based ketogenic diet. Fortunately, there are tons of healthy options that can provide the protein you need to keep you going.

A few examples of low-carb, plant-based proteins include:

• Tempeh

• Natto

• Nutritional Yeast

• Spirulina

• Nuts

• Seeds

High-quality, low-sugar plant-based protein powders

Similarly, nixing all dairy products from your diet can make it tricky to get in enough fat, but there are plenty of plant-based sources of fat available that can help you easily meet your needs.

Some of the healthiest plant-based fats include:

• Avocado Oil

• Coconut Oil

• Olive Oil

- MCT Oil

- Avocado

- Nuts

- Seeds

Note that you can easily swap these nutritious foods into your favorite recipes to make them completely plant-based and keto-friendly. Nutritional yeast, for example, makes a great substitute for cheese while tempeh can be crumbled and cooked like ground beef to make delicious veggie tacos or lettuce wraps.

Sample Meal Plan:

Wondering what exactly a plant-based ketogenic diet looks like? Here's a one-day sample meal plan that you can follow to help get you started!

Breakfast:

Gluten-free oatmeal (2 grams net carbs per serving)

Lunch:

Baked tempeh (3 grams net carbs per serving)

Cauliflower tabbouleh salad (6 grams net carbs per serving)

Olive oil vinaigrette (0 grams net carbs per serving)

Dinner:

Raw walnut tacos (4 grams net carbs per serving)

Super cilantro guacamole (5 grams net carbs per serving)

Snacks:

Keto smoothie with avocado, chia seeds & cacao (6.5 grams net carbs)

Almonds (2.5 grams net carbs per 1-oz serving)

Spicy roasted pumpkin seeds (10 grams carbs per 1-oz serving)

Daily Total: 39 grams net carbs

WHAT VEGASs EAT IN THEIR KETO JOURNEY

But can a vegetarian or vegan be Keto? Does the necessity of fat and the small margin for carbs eliminate anyone else except meat and dairy consumers? No. The vegetarian and vegan can still be LCHF while observing their food preferences. Here at Keys to Ketosis, we've provided a vegan ketogenic diet food list to help anyone who is conscious of what types of food they consume, but still wants to (or has to) pursue a low-carb, high-fat lifestyle.

Check out the list of compiled low-carb vegan diet below!

Tofu

The point of tension for a vegan/vegetarian attempting to pursue a LCHF will be the choices for a base food or "main course" food that will provide much of their protein and fat sources.

On the vegan ketogenic diet food list, tofu will be one of the big operators for finding interesting ways to creating mindful food that also assists you in your low-carb pursuit. Tofu is a versatile food, that comes in various forms and can be cooked in a variety of ways, including grilling, frying, baking, or just eating it raw. Having this on your vegan ketogenic diet food list will be imperative to maintaining excitement and variety.

Tofu Nutriton Facts (1/2 Cup):

Calories: 94

Fats: 6g

Carbs: 2.3g

Protein: 10g

Nuts

Nuts are a must on the Ketogenic diet, but peanuts should be eaten judiciously, due to their classification of legume, which means they belong to the same family as beans, and share their high carb profiles. However, you can use peanut butter for a topping, but once again, not in excess.

The good news for your vegan ketogenic diet food list is that there are plenty of nuts that are permissible – and beneficial – to being low-carb high-fat.

The best of the best include the following (in descending order from best to worst):

- Almonds

- Macadamia Nuts

- Walnuts

- Pecans

- Cashews and Pistachios

Nut based flours can also be used for baking instead of high-carb wheat flour.

MCT Oil

MCT Oil will make staying LCHF on a vegan diet easier than it has ever been.

MCT oil for keto diet plan

By using this supplement in shakes, as a dressing, or on other foods, you can ensure that your body is getting the correct doses of fatty acids that are essential to ketosis.

Other ideas:

Mixing in toppings (like mayo)

Use while baking food instead of regular baking oil

The great thing about using MCT Oil (and other exogenous ketones) is that you can counterbalance some of the carbs you will inevitably take by adhering to the vegan ketogenic diet food list.

Olive and Coconut Oil

Other oils that are great for toppings or cooking are coconut and olive oil. Both of these oils provide a great source of healthy fats, and a broad range of uses for food.

And unlike MCT Oil, these oils can be used for frying and sautéing food. Coconut oil is more stable than olive oil, so it is the better choice for using at high temperatures.

The benefit that these two oils bring to your vegan ketogenic diet food list, is their ability to provide vibrancy with flavor. While MCT Oil can provide a more potent shot of healthy fat, it can also bring with it a taste that can be hard to handle if not masked, whereas coconut and olive oil are both pleasurable to consume.

Greens

Since fruits are a no-no on the ketogenic diet (except for avocados), you will need to be strategic about eating enough greens to get the nutrients you'd get from the fruits you'd normally consume on a standard vegan diet.

The vegetables that you should keep stocked on your ketogenic diet food list are leafy greens like kale, collard greens, spinach, swiss chard, and others of the same family.

These vegetables, mixed with avocados and keto friendly oils (listed above) will help you stay vibrant from proper vitamin intake, while also helping you maintain a low-carb lifestyle.

Fatty Produce (Avocado)

The avocado is the hallmark of healthy fats from fruits (yes, avocados are a fruit). It is also capable of being used in every meal of the day, pairing well with salads. Did we mention that guacamole is incredible?

Avocados are considered a superfood, because of the research that suggests they help lower cholesterol, and even ward off cancer!

Nutrition Info (1 avocado):

Calories: 322

Fats: 29g

Carbs: 17g

Protein: 4g

CONCLUSION

What does it mean to be on a keto meal (often shortened to "keto") diet? When you're on a keto diet, you consume a very low-carb, high-fat diet. The idea behind this way of eating and why it can work so well is that when the body gets such small amounts of glucose from carbohydrates, it can burn another fuel source — fat — for energy. This is why the keto diet is known for helping the body to burn fat impressively fast! What if you're not trying to lower the number on your scale? The keto diet still may appeal to you since by limiting sugars and processed grains, you may lower your risk of developing type 2 diabetes, a disease which is becoming more and more common these days.

KETO MEAL PREP FOR BEGINNERS

INTRODUCTION

When the average person eats a meal rich in carbs, their body takes those carbs and converts them into glucose for fuel. Glucose is the body's main source of fuel when carbs are present in the body; on a Keto diet, there are very low if any at all carbs consumed, which forces the body to utilize other forms of energy to keep it functioning properly. This is where healthy fats come into play; with the absence of carbs, the liver takes fatty acids in the body and converts them into ketone bodies.

The ketogenic diet, or keto, is a diet that consists of very low carbs and high fat. That may sound too good to be true for many. Well, on this diet, this is a great day of eating and you can follow the rules perfectly with that meal plan.

A keto diet causes ketone bodies to be produced by the liver, and shifts the body's metabolism away from glucose in favor of fat-burning. A ketogenic diet restricts carbohydrates below a certain level (generally 100 per day). The ultimate determinant of whether a diet is ketogenic or not is the presence or absence of carbohydrates. Protein and fat intake vary. Contrary to popular belief, eating fat is not what causes ketosis. In the past, starvation diets were used often to induce ketosis

A lack of carbohydrates or presence of them ultimately determines if the diet is ketogenic.

In most eating plans, the body runs on a mixture of protein, fats, and carbohydrates. When carbohydrates are severely restricted and glycogen storage (glucose in muscle and liver) is depleted, the body begins to utilize other means to provide energy. FFA (free fatty acids) can be used to provide energy, but the brain and nervous system are unable to use FFA's. Although the brain can use ketone bodies for energy.

Ketone bodies are by products of incomplete FFA breakdown in the liver. Once they begin to accumulate fast and reach a certain level, they are released, accumulated in the bloodstream, and cause a state called ketosis. As this occurs, there is a decrease in glucose production and utilization. There is also less reliance on protein to meet energy requirements by the body. Ketogenic diets are often referred to as protein sparing, as they help to spare LBM while dropping body fat.

In regards to ketogenic diets, there are two primary hormones- insulin, glucagon that need to be considered. Insulin can be described as a storage hormone as its job is to take nutrients out of the bloodstream and carry them to target tissues. Insulin carries glucose from the blood to the liver and muscles, and it carries FFA from the blood into adipose tissue (stored fat triglyceride). On the other hand, glucagon breaks down glycogen stores (especially in the liver) and releases them into the blood.

When carbs are restricted or removed, insulin levels drop while glucagon levels rise. This causes an enhanced FFA release from fat cells, and increased FFA burning in the liver. This accelerated burning of FFA in the liver is what leads to ketosis. There are a number of other hormones involved with this process as well.

CHAPTER ONE

KETO MEAL PREPARATION

Obesity rates have skyrocketed; the incidence of diabetes has also increased, the main reason being that people's diets consist mainly of carbohydrates and fats, and the two don't mix well together; but protein and fats do mix well together. Watching your intake of carbohydrates is very important for weight loss. Low-carb diets or diets that teach food combining are very effective in weight loss. Ok, now for the myths.

The truth is that the father of low-carb, high-protein dates back to 1863, William Banting of England, who wrote a little booklet titled "Letter on Corpulence Addressed to the Public", William Banting is considered the father of low-carbohydrate dieting. He proved this over years, helping people lose weight without any side-effects.

The myth says that a low-carb, high-protein, and high-fat diet raises cholesterol; the truth is it actually lowers cholesterol.For one year, researchers at the Veterans Affairs Medical Center in Philadelphia followed 132 obese adults randomized into two groups. One restricted carbohydrate intake to less than 30 grams per day (low-carbohydrate diet); the other restricted caloric intake by 500 calories, with 30% of calories from fat (conventional diet).83% percent of the study group had diabetes or other risk factors for heart disease.

In the low-carb group, triglyceride levels decreased more and HDL ('good') cholesterol levels decreased less than in the low-fat group (high levels of triglycerides, a fat in the blood, are associated with heart disease). People with diabetes on the low-carb diet had a better control of blood sugar.

The low-carbohydrate group had more beneficial changes in triglyceride levels and HDL cholesterol levels than the low-fat diet group; the low-carb diet group also contained vitamins and other nutritional supplements.

Another myth says that a low-carb diet will raise your blood pressure; the truth is, with lower LDL levels and VLDL levels, blood pressure levels drop.

If people have high blood pressure and a weight problem, a low-carbohydrate diet might be a better option than a weight-loss medication.

Another myth says that you need carbohydrates or glucose for brain function; the truth is if you are on a hardcore low-carb, high-protein diet, where carbohydrates are non-existent, you are on what is called a Ketogenic Diet. When on such a strict diet, your body produces ketones in the absence of carbohydrates, then converts the ketones into a form of glucose that enables proper brain function.

Will I gain all my weight back if I stop my low-carb diet ?. That is totally false, it does not matter what diet you choose, if you are successful in your weight loss and then stop your diet, 9 out of 10 times you revert back to your old eating habits, and start eating junk and over-indulge, then of course you gain the weight back.

-Another myth: eating protein makes you fat. This is totally false; protein actually raises your calorie-burning metabolism by as much as 30% over carbohydrates. When proteins are consumed, your body must digest and break them down into amino acids, this takes energy and plenty of it, this actually helps you lose weight; not gain it.

Another myth: high-protein diets include fats, and fats are bad for me. Fats in the absence of carbohydrates burn more efficiently, and do not clog your arteries. As the studies show LDL's (low density lipoproteins) which are the artery cloggers, are lowered. The HDL's, which are the good carbohydrates, are raised even though your fat intake is increased, that, as mentioned above is attributed to low-carb intake. Carbs and fat don't mix, your body cannot efficiently break them down together, your liver is over-burdened and ends up converting the carbohydrates into fat, unless of course you are exercising like crazy.

Anotyher myth states: I will not have any energy with the low-carb diet. This is totally false, unless you are a marathon runner or bodybuilder. When you consume small amounts of carbohydrates, your body needs another source of energy; when glycogen levels are gone, your body starts using fat for energy and combustion. If you are extremely active, then it will take about 2-3 weeks, after that, your body is acclimated to your new eating habits and adjusts, energizing you as before. If you are involved in a endurance sport, then of course you need extra carbs to be competitive. If you are an athlete or work-out extensively, then you probably would not be dieting anyway, and a low-carb high-protein is a mute point.

Here are the most common myths associated to the low-carb diet plan.

1. It has been said that the low-carb diet will reduce the amount of calcium in your body. This couldn't be farther from the truth, as since the low-carb diet is rich in protein, this, in fact actually prevents calcium from entering your urine.

2. They say the low-carb diet plan will damage one's kidneys. Not unless one already has a kidney defect, because with the low-carb diet, though rich in protein, this is not what the entire meal is made of. Once on a low-carb diet, one still must observe the balancing of the meals consumed. It has been said that some doctors actually recommend a low-carb diet for some of their patients in order to treat kidney problems.

3. Moving from the kidneys, there's also this myth that while on a low-carb diet, you're dicing with heart disease. On the contrary, it's a fact that a low-carb diet plan actually reduces the risk of having heart disease. It has also been proven that even foods containing lots of animal fat and proteins do not constitute risk for heart disease.

4. There is no fibre present in the low-carb diet. The low carb diet is, on the contrary, full of fibre, and research also shows that the presence of this fibre actually lessens the effect and the amount of

carbohydrates in one's body. Which makes the low-carb diet a very pragmatic diet plan.

5. While on a low-carb diet, you're not allowed to consume fruits or vegetables. This is not true, because it's not a secret that the population for one reason or another just do not like eating fruits and vegetables. This goes back for years, and governments all over the world are now making it a point of duty by recommending the daily intakes. So, just because people have preferences doesn't mean it's down to the low-carb diet plan.

6. A low carb-diet means total elimination of carbohydrates. Even the most critical doctors, scientists, or nutritionists will dispel this, as in any given meal, one must have at least 45% - 65% carbohydrates in their meals, depending on each individual, of course.

7. Low-carb diets will produce permanent bad breath. This to some extent is true, but not because you're on a low-carb diet plan. This is simply because, people, regardless of what weight-loss or diet program they embark on, feel they have to abstain from other meals, such as eating fruits and vegetables. Even if one's not on any form of diet, not eating fruits and vegetables will certainly attract bad breath. To combat this is simple, just eat more fruits

and vegetables on a daily basis. This has nothing to do with a low-carb diet alone!

I hope with the above explanations, you can now take the plunge with ease and confidence and start embarking on a new and healthy journey and lifestyle using the low-carb diet plan.

Don't Be Confused About Low-Carb Diets

The high amounts of carbohydrates in our diet has led to increasing problems with obesity, diabetes, and other health problems. Critics, on the other hand, attribute obesity and related health problems to over-consumption of calories from any source, and lack of physical activity. Critics also express concern that the lack of grains, fruits, and vegetables in low-carbohydrate diets may lead to deficiencies of some key nutrients, including fiber, vitamin C, folic acid, and several minerals.

Any diet, whether low or high in carbohydrates, can produce significant weight-loss during the initial stages of the diet. But remember, the key to successful dieting is in being able to lose the weight permanently

- Differences Between Low-Carb Diets

There are many popular diets designed to lower carbohydrate consumption. Reducing total carbohydrates in the diet means that protein and fat will represent a proportionately greater amount of the total caloric intake.

The weight loss on low-carb diets is a function of caloric restriction and diet duration, and not reduced carbohydrate intake. This finding suggests that if you want to lose weight, you should eat fewer calories and do so over a long time period.

Little evidence exists on the long-range safety of low-carb diets. Despite the medical community's concerns, no short-term adverse effects have been found on cholesterol, glucose, insulin, and blood-pressure levels among participants on the diets. But, adverse effects may not show up because of the short period of the studies. Researchers note that losing weight typically leads to an improvement in these levels anyway, and this may offset an increase caused by a high-fat diet. The long-range weight change for low-carb and other types of diets is similar.

Low-carb diets do not enable the consumption of more calories than other kinds of diets, as has been often reported. A calorie is a calorie and it doesn't matter whether they come from carbohydrates or fat. Study discrepancies are likely the result of uncontrolled circumstances; i.e. diet participants that cheat on calorie consumption, calories burned during exercise, or any number of other factors. The drop-out rate for strict (i.e. less than 40 grams of CHO/day) low-carb diets is relatively high.

What Should You Do? - There are 3 important points I would like to re-emphasize:

- The long-range success rate for low-carb and other types of diets is similar.

- Despite their popularity, little information exists on the long-term efficacy and safety of low-carbohydrate diets.

- Strict low-carb diets are usually not sustainable as a normal way of eating. Boredom usually overcomes willpower.

The diet you choose should be a blueprint for a lifetime of better eating, not just a quick weight-loss plan to reach your weight goal. If you can't see yourself eating the prescribed foods longer than a few days or a week, then chances are it's not the right diet. To this end, following a moderately low-fat diet with a healthy balance of fat, protein, carbohydrates, and other nutrients is beneficial.

If you do decide to follow a low-carb plan, remember that certain dietary fats are associated with reduction of disease. Foods high in unsaturated fats that are free of trans-fatty acids such as olive oil, fish, flaxseeds, and nuts are preferred to fats from animal origins.

Another alternative to "strict" low-carb dieting would be to give up some of the bad carbohydrate foods but not "throw out the baby with the bath water". In other words, foods high in processed sugar, snacks, and white bread would be avoided, but foods high in complex carbohydrates such as fruit, potatoes, and whole grains, retained.

1. SESAME BROILED CHICKEN

Prep time: 5 minutes
Cook time: 20 minutes
Total time: 25 minutes

Ingredients:
4 bone-in, skin-on chicken thighs
¼ teaspoon salt
¼ teaspoon freshly ground black pepper
2 tablespoons soy sauce
2 tablespoons sugar-free maple syrup
1 tablespoon sesame oil
1 teaspoon minced garlic
1 teaspoon red wine vinegar
½ teaspoon crushed red pepper flakes

Direction:
Season the chicken with the salt and pepper. Set aside.
In a bowl large enough to hold the chicken, combine the soy sauce, maple syrup, sesame oil, garlic, vinegar, and red pepper flakes. Reserve about one quarter of the sauce.
Add the chicken thighs to the bowl, skin-side up. Submerge in the soy sauce. Refrigerate to marinate for at least 15 minutes.
Preheat the oven to broil.

Remove the chicken from the refrigerator. Place the thighs skin-side down in the baking dish.

Place the dish in the preheated oven, about six inches from the broiler. Broil for 5 to 6 minutes with the oven door slightly ajar. Turn the chicken skin-side up. Broil for about 2 minutes more.

Turn the chicken again so it is now skin-side down. Move the baking dish to the bottom rack of the oven. Close the oven door and broil for another 6 to 8 minutes.

Turn the chicken again to skin-side up. Baste with the reserved sauce. Close the oven door and broil for 2 minutes more.

Remove the chicken from the oven. With a meat thermometer, check the internal temperature.It should reach at least 165°F.

Cool the chicken for 5 minutes before serving.

2. GREEK EGG BAKE

Prep time: 5 minutes
Cook time: 25 minutes
Total time: 30 minutes

Ingredients:
12 eggs
1 cup kale, chopped
1/4 cup sun-dried tomatoes
1/2 cup feta
1/2 tsp oregano
Salt and pepper to taste
Greek egg bake recipe

Directions:
Pre-heat the oven to 350 degrees.
Whisk together eggs.
Add in kale, tomaotes, feta, and spice.
Line a baking pan with foil (makes it easier to remove from the pan).
Spray with non-stick spray.
Bake in the oven for about 25 minutes.
Slice and serve...or portion out for the week. Will keep in the fridge for 4-5 days.

3. TURMERIC SCRAMBLED EGG

Prep Time: 5 minutes
Cook time: 6 minutes
Ingredients:
4 large eggs
2 Tbsp. milk of choice
2 Tsp. dried turmeric
½ Tsp. dried parsley
salt& black pepper to taste
steamed veggie of choice
pre-cooked sausage of choice
turmeric eggs, broccoli, and sausage

Directions:
Spray a small frying pan with nonstick cooking spray and bring to a medium heat.
In a small bowl, whisk together the eggs, milk, turmeric, parsley, salt and pepper.
Transfer the eggs to the heated pan. Cook 2-3 minutes stirring constantly to break them apart.
Flip the eggs and cook another 2-3 minutes, or until desired.
Transfer the eggs to two meal prep containers, diving them evenly. Add steamed vegetables and sausage!

4. CAULIFLOWER HASH BROWNS

Prep time: 20 minutes
Cook time: 15 minutes
Total time: 45 minutes

Ingredients:
1 small head grated cauliflower (about 3 cups)
1 large egg
3/4 cup shredded cheddar cheese
1/4 tsp cayenne pepper (optional)
1/4 tsp garlic powder
1/2 tsp pink salt
1/8 tsp black pepper

Directions:
Grate entire head of cauliflower.
Microwave for 3 minutes and let cool. Place in paper towels or cheese cloth and wring out all the excess water.
Place wrung out cauliflower in a bowl, add rest of ingredients and combine well.
Form into six square shaped hash browns on a greased baking tray.
Place in a 400° oven for 15-20 minutes.
Let cool for 10 minutes and hash browns will firm up.
Serve warm. Enjoy!

5. BLUEBERRY PANCAKE BITES

Prep time: 15 minutes
Cook time: 25 minutes
Total time: 40 minutes

Ingredients:
4 large eggs
1/4 cup Swerve sweetener
1/2 tsp vanilla extract
1/2 cup [url]coconut flour
1/4 cup butter, melted
1 tsp baking powder
1/2 tsp salt
1/4 tsp cinnamon
1/3 to 1/2 cup water
1/2 cup Wyman's frozen wild blueberries

Directions:
Preheat oven to 325 F and grease a mini muffin tin (24 cavity) very well (double grease, first with butter and then with coconut oil spray).
In a blender combine the eggs, sweetener, and vanilla extract.Blend until smooth.
Add the coconut flour, melted butter, baking powder, salt, and cinnamon. Blend again until smooth. It will seem very liquidy but let it sit a few minutes and it will thicken up considerably. Add 1/3 cup of the water

and blend again. If it's still very thick, add a little additional water. You shouldn't be able to pour it, but you should be able to scoop it out of the blender easily.

Divide among the prepared muffin cups. Add a few blueberries to each. Press them gently into the batter. Bake 20 to 25 minutes, until set. Let cool a few minutes in the pan and then serve with your favourite low carb pancake syrup.

6. KETO BAGELS

Prep time: 15 minutes
Cook time: 14 minutes

Ingredients:
2 cups almond flour
1 tbsp baking powder
1 tsp garlic powder
1 tsp onion powder
1 tsp dried Italian seasoning
3 large eggs, divided
3 cups shredded low moisture mozzarella cheese
5 tbsp cream cheese
3 tbsp Everything Bagel Seasoning

Directions:
Preheat oven to 425°.Line a rimmed baking sheet with parchment paper or a Silpat.

In a medium mixing bowl, combine the almond flour, baking powder, garlic powder, onion powder, and dried Italian seasoning. Mix until well combined, put the mixture through a flour sifter to ensure that all the baking powder gets mixed in with the rest of the ingredients.

Crack one of the eggs into a small bowl and fork whisk. This will be the egg wash for the top of the bagels. The other two eggs will go in the dough.

In a large microwave safe mixing bowl, combine the mozzarella cheese and cream cheese. Microwave for 1 minute and 30 seconds. Remove from microwave and stir to combine. Return to microwave for 1 additional minute. Mix until well combined.

To the mixing bowl, add the remaining 2 eggs and the almond flour mixture. Mix until all ingredients are well incorporated. If the dough gets too stringy and unworkable, simply put it back in the microwave for 30 seconds to soften and continue mixing.

Divide the dough into 6 equal portions.Roll each portion into a ball.

Gently press your finger into the center of each dough ball to form a ring. Stretch the ring to make a small hole in the center and form it into a bagel shape.

Brush the top of each bagel with the egg wash.

Top each bagel with Everything Bagel Seasoning.

Bake on the middle rack for 12-14 minutes or until golden brown.

7. LOW-CARB BREAKFAST PIZZA

Prep time: 10 minutes
Cook time: 30 minutes
Total time: 40 minutes

Ingredients:
12 eggs
1/2 cup heavy cream
1/2 tsp salt
1/4 tsp pepper
8 oz sausage
2 cups peppers, sliced
1 cup cheese, shredded

Directions:
Preheat oven to 350°.
Add peppers to microwave for 3 minutes.
Brown sausage in cast iron skillet.
Take out and set aside.
Mix eggs, cream, salt and pepper together and add to skillet.
Cook for 5 minutes until the sides start to set up.
Add to oven and bake for 15 minutes.
Take out and add sausage, peppers and cheese.
Set under broiler for 3 minutes.

8. KETO BACON SAUSAGE MEATBALLS

Prep time: 10 minutes
Cook time: 30 minutes

Ingredients:
1 pound spicy italian sausage whole 30, if needed
9 sliced sugar-free bacon
2 tbsp garlic, minced
2 tbsp white onion diced
1 tbsp dried oregano

Directions:
Preheat oven to 375 F. Prepare a standard muffin pan by greasing 9 cavities lightly with coconut oil.
In a large mixing bowl, combine the Italian sausage, garlic, onion and oregano.
Roll the mixture into 9 equal balls with your hands and place on a plate.
Wrap each ball with a slice of bacon then place each one in a muffin cavity.
Bake at 375 F for 30 minutes then cook under a high broiler for 5 minutes to get the bacon crispy.
Remove from the oven and prepare.

9. CREAM CHEESE & SALAMI KETO PINWHEELS

Ingredients:
1 8oz block cream cheese
8-10 thin slices of pepperoni and genoa salami ,may need more depending on size
4 tbsp finely diced pickles

Directions:
Bring cream cheese to room temperature and whip until fluffy.
Spread cream cheese in a 1/4 inch thick rectangle in the center of a large piece of plastic wrap.
Spread pickles over cream cheese.
Place salami over cream cheese in overlapping layers so all cream cheese layer is covered.
Place a second piece of plastic wrap over salami layer and gently press down.
Flip entire rectangle over so bottom cream cheese layer is now facing the top.
Carefully peel back plastic wrap off top cream cheese layer.
Begin rolling into log shape slowly removing bottom layer of plastic wrap as you go.
Place pinwheel in tight plastic wrap and refrigerate at least 4 hours, overnight preferred.
Slice into preferred thickness.

10. CHEESEBURGER LETTUCE WRAPS

Prep time: 15 minutes
Cook time: 8 minutes
Total time: 23 minutes

Ingredients:
2 pounds lean ground beef
1/2 tsp seasoned salt
1 tsp black pepper
1 tsp dried oregano
6 slices American cheese
2 large heads iceburg or romaine lettuce, rinsed then dried
2 tomatoes, sliced thin
small red onion, sliced thin
Spread:1/4 cup light mayo
3 tbsp ketchup
1 tbsp dill pickle relish
dash of salt and pepper

Directions:
Heat a grill or skillet on medium heat.
In a large bowl, mix together ground beef, seasoned salt, pepper and oregano.
Divide mixture into 6 sections then roll each into a ball. Press each ball down flat to form a patty.

Place patties on grill/pan and cook for approximately 4 minutes on each side or until cooked to your liking. (If using a skillet, only cook 3 at a time to avoid over-crowding.)

Place a slice of cheese on each cooked burger. Place each burger on a large piece of lettuce. Top with spread , one slice tomato, red onion and whatever else you like. Wrap the lettuce up over the top and serve.

Spread: In a small bowl mix together all the spread ingredients. Refrigerate until ready to use.

11. SESAME SALMON WITH BABY BOK CHOY AND MUSHROOMS

Ingredients:
Main Dish
4 each 4-6 oz.salmon fillet
2 each portobello mushroom caps (or 8 oz. baby bella mushrooms)
4 each baby bok choy
1 tbsp toasted sesame seeds
1 each green onion
Marinade
1 tbsp olive oil
1 tsp sesame oil
1 tbsp coconut aminos
1/2 inch ginger grated (approx. 1 tsp.)
1/2 lemon juice
1/2 tsp salt
1/2 tsp black pepper

Directions:
Whisk together all of your marinade ingredients.
Drizzle half of the marinade on the salmon and turn to coat. Cover and refrigerate the salmon while it marinates for one hour.
Preheat oven to 400.

Prepare vegetables: Trim the rough ends from the bok choy and cut into halves. Slice the mushrooms into ½ inch pieces.

Drizzle the remaining marinade over the vegetables and lay on a lined baking sheet.

Place salmon, skin side down, on a lined baking sheet as well. Bake until salmon is cooked through, about 20 minutes.

Top with sliced green onions and sesame seeds.

12. BACON, CHICKEN & TOMATO STUFFED AVOCADO

Prep time: 10 minutes
Cook time: 20 minutes
Total time: 30 minutes

Ingredients:
2 chicken breasts, grilled
3 pieces bacon, cooked and chopped
2 avocado
1/3 cup grape tomatoes, chopped
1/3 cup mayo, paleo

Directions:
Sprinkle chicken with favorite seasoning, grill, and cut into cubes.
Grill bacon strips, and set aside.
Place cubed chicken in a medium bowl. Add tomatoes, onions and bacon.
Add Paleo Mayo and gently mix everything together.
Just before serving, slice avocados in half and discard pit.
Pile the chicken mix on top of each avocado half.

13. KETO CHICKEN ENCHILADA BOWL

Ingredients:
2-3 chicken breasts (about one pound of chicken)
3/4 cups red enchilada sauce
1/4 cup water
1/4 cup onion
1 4 oz can green chiles
1 12oz steam bag cauliflower rice

Preferred toppings- use avocado, jalapeno, cheese, and roma tomatoes, seasoning to taste.

Directions:
In skillet over medium heat cook chicken breasts until lightly brown.
Add enchilada sauce, chiles, onions, water and reduce heat to simmer, covered.
Cover and cook until chicken is cooked through and shred chicken.
Add chicken back into sauce and continue simmering for additional 10 minutes uncovered or until most of liquid has been soaked up.
Prepare cauliflower rice per bag instructions and dice preferred toppings.
Top rice with chicken, cheese, avocado or preferred toppings.

14. AVOCADO TUNA SALAD RECIPE

Prep time: 10 minutes

Ingredients
15 oz tuna in oil, drained and flaked (3 small cans)
1 English cucumber, sliced
2 large or 3 medium avocados peeled, pitted & sliced
1 small/medium red onion thinly sliced
1/4 cup cilantro (1/2 of a small bunch)
2 tbsp lemon juice freshly squeezed
2 tbsp extra virgin olive oil
1 tsp sea salt or to taste
1/8 tsp black pepper

Directions
In a large salad bowl, combine: sliced cucumber, sliced avocado, thinly sliced red onion, drained tuna, and 1/4 cup cilantro
Drizzle salad ingredients with 2 tbsp lemon juice, 2 tbsp olive oil, 1 tsp salt and 1/8 tsp black pepper (or season to taste). Toss to combine and serve.

15. SHEET PAN CHICKEN FAJITAS

Prep time: 15 minutes
Cook time: 20 minutes
Total time: 35 minutes

Ingredients:
1.5 lbs chicken breasts, boneless, skinless
olive oil
1 tbsp taco seasoning
3 bell peppers, sliced
1 onion, sliced thinly
fresh limes

Directions:
Preheat oven to 400ºF and grease large rimmed baking sheet.
Slice chicken into strips and season to coat with taco seasoning. Lightly drizzle seasoned chicken with olive oil.
Chop all veggies into strips. Drizzle with olive oil and more taco seasoning if desired.
Place chicken and veggies on sheet pan and bake at 400 F until chicken strips are cooked through and veggies are tender, about 20-25 minutes
Remove from oven and squeeze fresh lime over. Serve as desired in tortillas or over cauliflower rice.

16. SPICY MUSTARD THYME CHICKEN & COCONUT ROASTED BRUSSELS SPROUTS

Prep time: 10 minutes
Cook time: 25 minutes

Ingredients:
1 pound Brussels sprouts sliced in half
2 medium boneless skinless chicken breast
1/4 cup ground spicy mustard
1 tbsp lemon juice
1 tsp thyme
Salt & pepper to taste
1 tbsp coconut oil, melted

Directions:
In a small ramekin, whisk together the spicy mustard with lemon juice, salt, pepper, and thyme.

Place the two chicken breasts in a bowl and pour the mustard over them. Using a spoon, coat the chicken breasts with the mustard. Place in the refrigerator to marinate 10 minutes then remove and bring to room temperature 15 minutes prior to cooking.

Preheat oven to 350 F. Prepare a baking sheet with parchment paper.

Next, place Brussels sprouts in a medium bowl and toss with melted coconut oil, salt and pepper.

Transfer Brussels sprouts to the prepared baking sheets, spreading into an even layer.

Place marinated chicken breasts in a glass baking pan.

Place the chicken breasts in the oven baking at 350 F 10 minutes. After 10 minutes, place the Brussels sprouts in the oven.Cook both 15 minutes.

Remove from the oven and divide the meal into two servings, placing in individual meal prep containers.

17. FATHEAD PIZZA CRUST RECIPE
(LOW-CARB KETO PIZZA)

Prep time: 10 minutes

Cook time: 10 minutes

Total time: 20 minutes

This low carb keto Fathead pizza crust recipe with coconut flour is so easy, with only 4 ingredients, it's the ultimate keto pizza - easy to make, chewy, and ready in 20 minutes.

Ingredients:

1 1/2 cup mozzarella cheese, shredded

2 tbsp cream cheese cut into cubes

2 large eggs, beaten

1/3 cups coconut flour

Directions:

Preheat the oven to 425° F . Line a baking sheet or pizza pan with parchment paper.

Combine the shredded mozzarella and cubed cream cheese in a large bowl. Microwave for 90 seconds, stirring halfway through. Stir again at the end until well incorporated (**see notes for an alternative to the microwave).

Stir in the beaten eggs and coconut flour. Knead with your hands until a dough forms. If the dough becomes hard before fully mixed, you can microwave for 10-15 seconds to soften it.

Spread the dough onto the lined baking pan to 1/4" or 1/3" thickness, using your hands or a rolling pin over a piece of parchment (the rolling pin works better if you have one). Use a toothpick or fork to poke lots of holes throughout the crust to prevent bubbling.

Bake for 6 minutes. Poke more holes in any places where you see bubbles forming. Bake for 3-7 more minutes, until golden brown.

Recipe notes:

To make a keto pizza, top with sauce and toppings after cooking the crust and return to the oven for about 10 minutes, until heated through.

**If you don't want to use the microwave, use a double boiler to melt the cheese and cream cheese together instead. Boil water in a saucepan, then place the cheeses in a metal bowl resting over the edges of the saucepan. The idea is to melt the cheese without burning it, stirring frequently.

Nutrition info does not include toppings.

18. KETO LASAGNA WITH ZUCCHINI NOODLES

Prep time: 15 minutes
Cook time: 30 minutes
Total time: 45 minutes

Ingredients:
16 oz ground beef
1 cup Rao's marinara sauce
1 zucchini, large
10 oz ricotta cheese
4 oz mozzarella cheese, shredded

Directions:
Preheat oven to 350° F. Peel zucchini into strips and leave out the seedy core. Salt and let sit for 15 minutes and blot with paper towels.
Brown ground beef in pan and add marinara. Season well with salt and pepper.
Layer into a small casserole dish: meat, zucchini, ricotta, meat, zucchini, ricotta, mozzarella.
Cover with foil and bake for 30 minutes. Broil uncovered for 2-3 minutes to brown the top.

19. ONE-PAN LEMON CHICKEN WITH ASPARAGUS

Prep time: 5 minutes
Cook time: 25 minutes
Total time: 30 minutes
The method here is simple enough: coat your chicken in light flour batter. You can use a regular gluten free flour or tapioca/arrowroot if you're looking for a grain free.

After you brown the chicken on both sides, you quickly braise the asparagus in the pan along with a little garlic, stock, lemon juice and mustard. Once the sauce reduces down you simply add the chicken back to the pan, sprinkle with some parsley for added freshness and you're done. All done in less than 30 minutes and in one pan.

Serve the lemon chicken & asparagus over a bed of rice/cauliflower rice to soak up all the saucy goodness. Bright and punchy lemon garlic flavours with a tangy, mustard bite .

Ingredients:
4 chicken breasts, boneless, skinless
1/4 cup tapioca flour for paleo or plain gluten-free flour
2 tbsp olive oil
3/4 tsp sea salt plus more for seasoning
1/2 tsp ground black pepper plus more for seasoning

1 pound asparagus stalks ends trimmed and then cut in half
2 cloves garlic crushed
3 tbsp fresh lemon juice
1/2 zest of lemon
1 tbsp dijon mustard
1 cup chicken stock aim for a lower sodium stock
1 tbsp fresh parsley roughly chopped, plus more for garnishing

Directions:

Place the chicken breasts between two pieces of plastic cling wrap and pound them down to make them even in thickness. This will help the chicken cook evenly and make for more tender chicken. If your breasts are extra thick you can also just cut/slice them in half.

Place the flour, salt & pepper in a shallow dish and gently toss the chicken breasts to coat in flour.

In a large skillet add one tablespoon of olive oil and bring to a medium-high heat. When the oil is hot add the chicken to the skillet and cook each side for about 5 minutes or until golden and cooked through. Once cooked remove the chicken and place on a paper towel lined plate. Set aside while you cook the asparagus.

Add the remaining 1 tablespoon olive oil in the skillet. Add the asparagus stalks and sauté for a minute. Add the garlic and sauté another minute longer until fragrant.

In a small bowl or cup whisk together the lemon juice and mustard until fully mixed.Pour into the skillet with the asparagus along with the chicken stock and the zest. Bring the liquid to a boil and then reduce down to a simmer. Cover and let cook another 3-4 minutes or until the asparagus is tender.

Stir in the parsley and then add the chicken back to the pan and rotate the breasts to coat in the liquids. Taste the sauce and season with more salt & pepper as needed.

20 .CHEESY BACON-STUFFED MINI PEPPERS

Prep time: 15 minutes
Cook time: 12 minutes
Total time: 27 minutes
These Cheesy Bacon-Stuffed Mini Peppers are the perfect crowd pleasing appetizer. They're stuffed with two kinds of cheese, bacon, and more, then baked till melty and delicious!

Ingredients:
6 mini sweet peppers sliced in half, seeds and membranes removed
4 oz cream cheese
2 tbsp green onions, sliced
4 slices bacon, cooked and crumbled
1/2 tsp garlic powder
1/2 cup shredded cheddar cheese, plus extra for topping
1 tsp Worcestershire sauce
chopped cilantro for topping (optional)

Directions:
Preheat oven to 400°. Spray a cookie sheet with nonstick cooking spray and set aside.
In a small bowl, beat together the cream cheese, green onions, bacon, garlic powder, cheddar, and

worcestershire sauce with an electric mixer until smooth.

Fill the sliced peppers with the filling, about a heaping tablespoon each. Place on prepared cookie sheet, then sprinkle each pepper with a little extra cheese. Bake in the preheated oven for 10-12 minutes until cheese is melted and bubbly and peppers have softened.

Allow to cool slightly before eating. Sprinkle with a little chopped cilantro if desired.

21. STEAK BITES

Prep time: 10 minuts
Cook time: 3 minuts
Marinate time: 3-24 hours

Ingredients:
1/2 cup soy sauce
1/3 cup olive oil
1/4 cup Worcestershire sauce
1 tsp minced garlic
2 tbsp dried basil
1 tbsp dried parsley
1 tsp black pepper
1-1/2 lbs flat iron or top sirloin steak, cut in 1-inch pieces

Directions:
Place all ingredients, except steak, in a large ziplock baggie. Stir with a spoon to combine.
Drop steak pieces in and seal shut. Shake gently to coat steak entirely in marinade.Place bag in refrigerator to marinate for at least 3 hours or up to 24.
Heat a large skillet over medium-high heat. Heat skillet until it's very hot. Remove steak pieces from marinade using a slotted spoon and place in hot skillet. Discard marinade. Cook steak according to your desired temperature.We like medium-well so I cooked ours for about 3 minutes.

22. KETO AVOCADO BROWNIES

Prep time: 10 minutes
Cook time: 35 minutes
Total time: 45 minutes

Ingredients:
250 g avocado about 2
1/2 tsp vanilla
4 tbsp cocoa powder
1 tsp stevia powder
3 tbsp refined coconut oil
2 eggs
100 g Lily's Dark Chocolate, melted
90 g blanched almond flour
1/4 tsp baking soda
1 tsp baking powder
1/4 tsp salt
1/4 cup erythritol

Directions:
Preheat the oven to 350F.
Peel the avocados and place in a food processor. Process until smooth.
Add each ingredient one at a time and process for a few seconds until all of the ingredients (except the dry ones) have been added to the food processor.

In a separate bowl, combine the dry ingredients together and whisk together. Add to the food processor and mix until combined.

Place a piece of parchment paper over a 30x20cm baking dish and pour the batter into it. Spoon evenly and place in the preheated oven. Bake for 35 minutes.

Take out of the oven, let cool and slice into 12 pieces.

23. COCONUT OIL FAT BOMBS

Prep time: 15 minutes
Cook time: 5 minutes
Total time: 20 minutes

These 5-ingredient coconut oil bombs melt in your mouth and pack a dose of energy!

Ingredients:
 2 cups shredded unsweetened coconut
 1/3 cup coconut oil, melted
 2 tbsp raw honey
 4 oz raw dark chocolate chips
 1/2 tsp vanilla bean powder, optional

Directions:
In a blender, add shredded coconut, coconut oil, raw honey and vanilla bean powder. Blend until mixture is fine and crumbled.
Line a small baking sheet or plate with wax paper. Using a tablespoon-size measuring spoon, scoop mixture and form into small mounds, using your hands. Set onto wax paper.Place in freezer 10 minutes to set. Using a double boiler, melt chocolate until smooth. Use a butterknife to drizzle coconut bombs with chocolate. Place back into refrigerator to set 10 minutes. Store in refrigerator.

24. KETO BREAD

Total time: 40 minutes

Ingredients:
1½ cups almond flour
6 egg whites
¼ tsp cream of tartar
3–4 tbsp butter, melted
¾ tsp baking soda
3 tsp apple cider vinegar
2 tbsp coconut flour

Directions:
Preheat oven to 375 F.
The first thing you'll need to do is separate six eggs. You'll only use the egg whites for this keto bread recipe, so feel free to set the yolks off to the side to save for another recipe. Add the cream of tartar to the egg whites and, using a hand mixer, whip the eggs until soft peaks are formed.
Add the almond flour, butter, baking soda, apple cider vinegar and coconut flour to a food processor, blending until well-incorporated.
Place the mix into a bowl and gently fold in the egg white mixture.
Grease an 8x4 loaf pan and pour in the bread mixture.

Bake for 30 minutes.

Your loaf should come out just browned on top!

Allow the bread to cool slightly before cutting into it.

Then, serve and enjoy!

25. AVOCADO DEVILED EGGS RECIPE — THE IDEAL KETO SNACK

Total time: 25 minutes

Ingredients:
4–6 eggs
1 avocado
¼ tsp sea salt
¼ tsp pepper
¼ tsp garlic
¼ tsp chili powder
¼ tsp cumin
¼ tsp smoked paprika, optional*
2 tbsp cilantro

Directions:
In a medium pot add eggs and cover with water until fully submerged.
Bring to a boil, then remove from heat and cover for 12–13 minutes.
Fill a large bowl with ice water and, using a slotted spoon, gently place eggs in the bowl, allowing eggs to chill for 5 minutes.
Remove outer casing from eggs and slice in half lengthwise, removing the yolk.
Add the yolk, along with the avocado and spices to a bowl, mixing together until well combined.

Add the mixture to the egg halves.

Drizzle with lime juice and top with cilantro.

Benefit-rich eggs are a serious powerhouse food. They're a relatively inexpensive source of meat-free protein that can help prevent disease, improve eye health and help you drop pounds. And while they're most often enjoyed as a breakfast food or a baking ingredient, they make a pretty tasty and popular appetizer in the form of deviled eggs.

26. CHOCOLATE FAT BOMBS RECIPE

Prep time: 10 minuts
Total time: 25 minuts

Ingredients:
125g/4.4 oz cream cheese
125g/4.4 oz unsalted butter
2 tbsp cacao powder
1 tbsp sweetener of choice (or more to taste)

Directions:
Place the cream cheese and butter into a large bowl and allow to soften gently at room temperature.
When softened beat briefly with an electric whisk then add the cacao powder and your sweetener of choice.
Beat until smooth.
Get out mini baking cups and place 1-2 teaspoons of the mixture into each cup.
Place into the fridge to firm and enjoy!

27. CAULIFLOWER-CRUSTED GRILLED CHEESE SANDWICHES

Ingredients:
1 medium head of cauliflower (raw), cut into small florets and stems removed
1 large egg
1/2 cup shredded Parmesan cheese
1 tsp Italian herb seasoning
2 thick slices of white cheddar cheese (you can also use shredded cheddar cheese)

Directions:
Preheat oven to 450F. Place cauliflower into food processor and pulse until crumbs about half the size of a grain of rice.

Place cauliflower into large microwave safe bowl and microwave for 2 minutes. Your cauliflower should be soft and tender (and hot!). (If you don't want to use the microwave to dry out the cauliflower and prefer to steam and wring with a cloth to dry.)

Stir cauliflower to mix up the bottom and top cauliflower. Place back into the microwave and cook for another 3 minutes. Remove and stir again so that all the cauliflower cooks evenly. Place back into microwave and cook for 5 minutes. At this point, you should see the cauliflower is starting to become more dry. Microwave for another 5 minutes. Cauliflower should still be slightly moist to the touch, but should look dry and clumped up, If you've made cauliflower pizza or breadsticks with the cloth wringing dry method,

Allow cauliflower to cool for a few minutes. Then add in egg and cheese. Stir to combine until smooth paste forms. Stir in seasoning. Divide dough into 4 equal parts. Place onto large baking sheet lined with parchment paper.Using your knuckles and fingers, shape into square bread slices about 1/3 inch thick.Bake cauliflower bread for about 15-18 minutes or until golden brown. Remove from oven and let cool a few minutes.

Using a good spatula, carefully slide cauliflower bread off of parchment paper. Now you are ready to assemble your sandwiches. You can do this a few different ways. You can either cook on the stove top as you would normally cook a grilled cheese. You can also place sandwiches into toaster oven and broil for several minutes (5-10) until cheese is completely melted and bread is toasty. If you don't own a toaster oven, you can also do this in the oven.

28. CHICKEN PAD THAI

Prep time: 20 minutes
Cook time: 10 minutes
Total time: 30 minutes

This chicken pad thai recipe is extremely healthy and nutritious meal, it can be prepared ahead of time.

Ingredients:
⅛ tsp ground ginger
⅛ tsp garlic powder
⅛ tsp sea salt
⅛ tsp freshly ground black pepper
2 pounds free-range chicken tenders
2 tbsp peanut oil
3 large free-range eggs, lightly beaten
⅓ cup organic chicken broth
3 tbsp peanut butter
2 tbsp tamari
1 tbsp rice vinegar
½ cup chopped scallion
2 garlic cloves, minced
1 tsp red pepper flakes
4 zucchini, spiralized
½ cup bean sprouts
½ cup crushed peanuts, for garnish
1 lime, cut into wedges, for garnish

Directions:

In a medium bowl, mix the ginger, garlic powder, salt, and black pepper. Add the chicken tenders and toss until coated.

In a medium skillet, heat the peanut oil over medium-high heat. When the oil is hot, add the chicken tenders and cook, turning once, until cooked through, about 3 minutes. Remove the chicken from the skillet and cut into ¼-inch-thick slices.Set aside.

Add the eggs to the skillet and scramble them for about 1 minute. Remove the scrambled eggs from the skillet and set aside.

Reduce the heat under the skillet to medium-low and add the chicken broth, peanut butter, tamari, vinegar, scallion, garlic, and red pepper flakes. Stir well and cook for 3 minutes.

Add the chicken slices, zucchini noodles, scrambled eggs, and sprouts to the skillet. Toss to coat with the sauce, and cook for about 1 minute.

Serve the pad thai garnished with the peanuts and lime wedges.

29. CINNAMON BUTTER FAT BOMBS

Ingredients:

1 lb salted butter, preferably grass-fed

1/4 cup honey (OR, substitute all or part of the honey with your favorite low-calorie sweetener to taste; personally I like 1 tablespoon honey and 20 drops SweetLeaf clear liquid stevia)

1 tbsp cinnamon

1 1/2 tsp vanilla extract

Salt to taste, if using unsalted butter

Directions:

Allow butter to soften on your counter until it is slightly squishy.

Add butter, cinnamon, honey/stevia, and vanilla extract to your food processor. Process for a couple of minutes to mix ingredients and achieve slightly whipped taste. Stop food processor as necessary to scrape down the bowl and reincorporate ingredients.

Spoon butter mixture into silicone molds, Alternatively, you can line a cutting board or other flat surface with parchment paper and then spoon dollops of butter mixture onto the parchment paper.

Freeze for an hour or two, then remove from parchment paper or molds and store in a container in your freeze.

30. COCONUT OIL MAYONNAISE

Total time: 10 minutes

Ingredients:
2 egg yolks at room temperature
1 tsp mustard
2 tsp fresh lemon juice
½ cup olive oil
¾ cup of coconut oil, melted
pinch of sea salt and black pepper

Directions:
In a blender, add egg yolks, mustard, 1 teaspoon fresh lemon juice and blend on very low setting.
Slowly drizzle in the oil while blender is still on low speed.
Once oil is well incorporated, add the remaining lemon juice.
Add salt and pepper, to taste.
Place mayo in a jar and store in the refrigerator.

31. CREAMY CAULIFLOWER MASH AND KETO GRAVY

Total time: 1 hour

Ingredients:
5 cups cauliflower chopped
4 tbsp heavy whipping cream
3 tbsp Butter
5 cloves garlic minced
2 tsp dried rosemary
3 tbsp parmesan
1/2 tsp pepper
Pink salt (to taste)

Directions:
Chop up 5 cups of raw cauliflower.
Bring pot of water to a boil (enough to cover all the cauliflower), add the cauliflower and boil for 15 minutes or until tender.
Drain cauliflower and place in processor.
Cook butter, garlic and rosemary in a saucepan over medium heat until fragrant.
Add melted butter, garlic and rosemary to processor and pulse several times until well combined.
Add cream, parmesan, salt and pepper to processor and process until smooth and creamy.
Taste for salt level. Serve warm.

32. CRUSTLESS SPINACH QUICHE RECIPE

Total time: 40 minutes

Ingredients:
1 tbsp coconut oil
1 onion, chopped
1 package frozen chopped spinach, thawed and drained
8 eggs, beaten
3 cups shredded raw cheese
¼ tsp sea salt
⅛ tsp black pepper

Directions:
Preheat oven to 350° F and grease a 9 inch pie pan with coconut oil.

Heat coconut oil, and onions over medium heat in sauce pan until onions are soft. Stir in spinach and cook until excess moisture has evaporated.

In a bowl, combine eggs, cheese, salt and pepper. Add spinach mixture and blend.

Scoop into pan and bake for 30 minutes.

33. SIMPLE PALEO CHICKEN CURRY RECIPE

Prep time: 30 minutes
Cook time: 30 minutes

Ingredients:
2 tbsp coconut oil (or oil of your choice)
8 chicken thighs ,boneless skinless, cut into 1" pieces
1 large onion, cut into large chunks
3 small zucchini, cut half lengthwise and thickly sliced
1 tsp garlic, minced
1 tbsp curry powder
1/2 tsp paprika
2 tsp salt
2 cans coconut milk (about 15 oz each)
1 cup tomatoes
cilantro (to garnish)

Directions:
Heat the olive oil in a stock pot to high heat. Add the chicken and cook until chicken pieces are browned on both sides. Remove the chicken from the pan and set aside, keeping the remaining oil in the stock pot.
Add the onion and zucchini and saute until lightly browned. Add the garlic, curry powder, paprika, and salt and saute for 30 seconds.
Add the chicken back into the pot, along with the coconut milk. Bring to a boil.

Reduce heat to a simmer, cover the pot with a lid, and let simmer for 30 minutes, or until chicken is tender. Add the tomatoes to the pot in the last 5 minutes of cooking.

Serve in a bowl with the coconut broth, like a soup.Top with cilantro.

34. CAULIFLOWER MAC AND CHEESE

Total time: 30-40 minutes

Ingredients:
1 large cauliflower head, cut into small florets
½-¾ cup kefir
½ cup goat's milk cottage cheese, pureed
1½ tsp Dijon mustard
1½ cups grated sheep's or goat's milk cheddar cheese, plus additional for topping
½ tsp black pepper
1 tsp sea salt
⅛ tsp garlic powder

Directions:
Preheat oven to 375° F. Grease 8" x 8" pan with ghee.
Bring a pot of salted water to a boil. Add cauliflower and cook until slightly tender, about 5 minutes. Drain and pat dry with paper towels. Spread in prepared pan.
In a saucepan over medium-high heat, mix together kefir, cottage cheese, and mustard until smooth.
In a saucepan over medium high heat, mix together the cottage cheese, kefir and mustard until smooth
Stir in cheese, sea salt, black pepper, and garlic powder until cheese just starts to melt. Pour over cauliflower and stir. Top with additional cheese if desired and bake for 10–15 minutes.

35. JALAPENO CHEDDAR BURGERS
(TURKEY OR BEEF)

Prep time: 15 miunutes
Cook time: 15 minutes
Total time: 30 minutes

Ingredients:
28 oz lean turkey or beef (not extra lean)
2 tbsp finely minced onion
salt & pepper to taste
4 tbsp cream cheese
2 oz shredded cheddar cheese
1/4 tsp garlic powder
1 fresh jalapeno pepper, diced (seeds removed if you prefer less spice)
1 tbsp olive oil
Rolls & Toppings as desired

Directions:
Preheat grill to medium or oven to broil on high.
In a small bowl combine cream cheese, cheddar cheese, garlic powder and diced jalapeno.
Combine meat, salt & pepper and minced onion. Divide meat into 4 even pieces (7oz each). Take 1/4 of the cream cheese mixture and flatten it into a pancake shape. Wrap beef or turkey around the cheese ensuring the cheese mixture is completely

covered. Brush each burger with a little bit of olive oil.

To Grill:

Grill burgers over medium heat for 6-7 minutes on each side or until completely cooked. (Turkey should reach an internal temperature of 165 degrees and beef should reach 160° F.)

To Broil:

Place burgers on a foil covered pan approximately 6" from the broiler. Broil 5-6 minutes on each side or until completely cooked. (Turkey should reach an internal temperature of 165° and beef should reach 160° F.)

36. ONION SOUP

Total time: 45–60 minutes

Ingredients:
4 large onions, peeled and thinly sliced
2 cups chicken bone broth
2 cups beef bone broth
4 tbsp ghee
5 garlic cloves, chopped
Goat cheese, for topping (optional)
Sea salt and black pepper to taste

Directions:
In a stock pot over medium heat, melt ghee and thinly sliced onions.
Cook onions until lightly caramelized.
Add bone broth and garlic.
Season with salt and pepper to taste.
Bring mixture to a boil and then reduce the heat and allow to simmer for 30–50 minutes (the longer, the more flavor).
Soup, glorious soup. It's such an easy way to start a multi-course meal or, paired with a side salad and sprouted bread, a simple lunch or dinner. And there's no better — or easier — soup than this onion soup recipe. You've likely had French onion when out, or maybe even from a can, but no more. With this easy onion soup recipe, you can enjoy homemade, healthy onion soup whenever the mood strikes.

37. BABA GANOUSH

Prep time: 20 minutes
Total time: 30 minutes

Ingredients:
1 eggplant, sliced
1 cup tahini
3–4 garlic cloves, smashed
1–2 tbsp avocado oil
1 cup parsley, chopped
Sea salt and pepper to taste

Directions:
On a baking sheet lined with parchment paper, lay out the eggplant slices.
Salt the eggplant and allow eggplant to sit for 15–20 minutes to remove moisture.
Use a paper towel to dab eggplant, removing excess water.
Broil eggplant on top oven rack for 5–8 minutes.
Remove skin (optional).
Place eggplant in a food processor and pulse until broken down.
Place all other ingredients in the food processor and blend on high until well combined.
Serve with chopped vegetables.

38. PIZZA GRILLED CHICKEN

Prep time: 15 minutes
Cook time: 15 minutes
Total time: 25 minutes

Ingredients:
1 boneless skinless chicken breast
1/2 tbsp olive oil
1 clove garlic, minced
1/2 cup half & half or heavy whipping cream
1/4 tsp xanthan gum thickener
1 cup fresh spinach, roughly chopped
1/2 cup part-skim shredded mozzarella
Sea salt & pepper to taste

Fathead Dough:
2oz cream cheese
3/4 cup shredded mozzarella
1 egg, beaten
1/4 tsp garlic powder
1/3 cup almond flour

Directions:
To make the pizza crust,
Melt mozzarella and cream cheese in the microwave
for 30 seconds at a time. Mixing often.

In a separate bowl mix beaten egg with almond flour and remaining dough ingredients.

Combine cheese mixture with flour and mix. Mix. Keep mixing! Once a sticky dough consistency has been reached, refrigerate while preparing sauce and chicken.

Saute the chicken in a skillet over medium heat until done.Remove, set aside.

Add garlic plus the xantham gum with half & half to the skillet and bring to a boil. Reduce to simmer when sauce starts to thicken.

Fold in spinach, cook just until wilted.

Using hands, work dough out into a circle on a pizza pan. Bake on 350 for 10 minutes. Crust must be pre-baked to hold up to the sauce and toppings.

Spread sauce/spinach mixture onto your cooked pizza crust. Top with chicken and shredded cheese

Bake 5 minutes or until cheese is melted.

NOTE* if your oven and pizza crust weren't already hot from making the dough, bake for 10 minutes instead.

39. BURGER COOK MUSHROOOM

Ingredients:

1 pound grass fed beef

24 baby portabella mushrooms

4 slices sharp cheddar, sliced into quarters

4 tbsp chopped yellow onion

2 dill pickles, sliced

2 tbsp extra virgin olive oil

12 basil leaves

yellow mustard, mayo, sriracha or low carb ketchup (optional)

salt and pepper to taste

Directions:

Remove stems from portabella mushroom caps and wipe with a damp paper towel to remove any dirt or debris. In a small saucepan, heat 1 tablespoon olive oil over medium heat. Add mushroom caps and cook for 2 minutes on each side, allowing mushrooms to cook through but retain firmness.

Remove mushrooms from pan and place on paper towels to allow liquid to drain off.

Divide the ground beef into 12 portions, rolling each into a small disc shape. Add salt and pepper to taste. In a large grill pan, heat remaining tbsp olive oil over medium heat. Once the pan is hot, add the meat and allow to cook for 3 minutes on one side. Flip and allow to cook for 3 minutes on the other side. Cook to desired level of doneness.

Stack a mushroom, burger, cheese, onion, pickles and your choice of condiments. Top with second mushroom cap and add a basil leaf for garnish. Use a toothpick to hold.

40. EASY CHOCOLATE MOUSSE

Ingredients:
8 oz cream cheese block, softened
¼ cup unsweetened cocoa powder
½ large avocado, pitted
⅛ tsp vanilla extract
2-3 tbsp of desired sweetener, I recommend Swerve.
¼ cup heavy whipping cream
90% dark chocolate, shaved for garnish

Directions:
Beat together the cream cheese until creamy and smooth using a handheld mixer in a medium mixing bowl. Slowly mix in the cocoa powder. Beat in the avocado and mix until creamy smooth, approximately 5 minutes.

Add the vanilla extract and sweetener and beat again until smooth, approximately 1-2 minutes.

In a separate mixing bowl, whip the heavy cream until stiff peaks form.

Place the whipped cream in the chocolate mixture and gently fold until it's incorporated.

Place the chocolate mousse in a piping bag and pipe into desired containers. Garnish with dark chocolate shavings.

41. LOW-CARB TACOS

Prep time: 30 minutes
Cook time: 30 minutes
Total time: 1 hour

Ingredients:
Cheese Taco Shells:
2 cups cheddar cheese, shredded

Taco Meat:
1 lb ground beef
1 tbsp chili powder
2 tsp cumin
1 tsp onion powder
1/2 tsp garlic powder
1/4 tsp salt
1/4 cup water
Toppings for taco: Sour cream, avocado, cheese, lettuce, etc.

Directions:
Preheat oven to 350F.
On a baking sheet lined with parchment paper or a silicone mat place 1/4 cup piles of cheese 2 inches apart. Press the cheese down lightly so it makes one layer.

Place baking sheet in the oven and bake for 5-7 minutes or until the edges of the cheese are brown.

Let the cheese cool for 2-3 minutes then lift it up and place it over the handle of a spoon or other utensil that is balanced on two cups.

Let cheese cool completely then remove.

While you continue to bake your cheese taco shells place the ground beef in a skillet over medium high heat cooking until it is completely cooked through.

Drain the grease from the meat and then add the cumin, chili powder, onion, powder, garlic powder, and salt. Pour water into skillet and stir everything around mixing it together.

Simmer for 5 minutes or until liquid has cooked away.

Add meat to taco shells and top with your favorite taco toppings.

42. ALFREDO RECIPE

Total time: 15 minutes

Ingredients:
1 small head of cauliflower, chopped (about 3 heaping cups)
2 tbsp olive oil
2 cloves garlic, smashed and minced
2 tsp pine nuts
2¼ cup almond milk
2 tsp of each: salt, pepper, oregano, and basil
juice of half a lemon
¼ cup plus 1 tbsp nutritional yeast

Directions:
In a medium-sized pot, cook the olive oil, garlic and pine nuts over medium heat for 3–4 minutes, or until garlic is golden brown.
Add in the almond milk and bring to a boil.
Reduce heat to medium and add the cauliflower and spices and cook until cauliflower is soft (about 8 minutes).
Transfer to a high-powered blender and add in the lemon juice and nutritional yeast and blend on high until smooth.
Add over your favorite gluten-free pasta or zoodles and top with fresh basil.

43. LOW-CARB BLUEBERRY MUFFINS

Ingredients:
½ stick (2 oz) butter, very soft
4 tbsp (2 oz) cream cheese, very soft
1/2 tsp vanilla
½ cup coconut flour
¼ cup Swerve Granulated
1 tsp baking powder
1/4 tsp salt
1/16 tsp cinnamon
1/8 tsp xanthan gum
3 large eggs
1/4 cup heavy cream
1/3 cup fresh blueberries
2 tsp Swerve Granulated

Directions:
Preheat oven to 350° . Position oven rack to the lower third of the oven. Line a 6-cup muffin tin with paper liners. Add the dry ingredients together in a smaller bowl and whisk together to combine and break up any lumps.

In a medium bowl, cream the butter, cream cheese, and vanilla together until light and fluffy. Add 1 egg and beat into the butter mixture until the mixture is light and fluffy (it may break or separate, it's okay). Add 1/3 of the dry ingredients and mix until completely incorporated, making sure to keep that light, fluffy texture. Keep in mind that we want a light and fluffy − almost mousse-like texture throughout this process.

Add another egg and beat until fully combined and the batter is fluffy. Add half of the remaining dry ingredients, beating again. Add the last egg, beating until fully incorporated, followed by the last of the dry ingredients. Finish by adding the heavy cream, once again, beating until the batter is thick, but still light and fluffy.Fold in the blueberries.

Spoon the thick batter into a plastic zip-loc bag and snip off a corner, producing about a 3/4 inch hole. Place the snipped corner into a muffin liner and squeeze the batter into a fat, rounded mound, filling the muffin liner about 3/4 full. Repeat for each muffin liner, adding any remaining batter to those that need a little more. Knock down any peaks with your finger. Sprinkle about ¼ teaspoon of Swerve granulated over the top of each muffin to help prevent burning and to give the muffins a nice look.

Place the muffins into the oven. Turn the oven up to 400° degrees for 5 minutes. Then, turn the oven back to 350° and bake the blueberry muffins for about 25 minutes more. They're ready when they feel firm when lightly pressed with a finger, but still sound a little moist. Remove from the oven and let cool five minutes before gently removing from the pan and placing on a cooling rack.

44. KETO BEEF WITH BROCCOLI

Prep time: 15 minutes
Cook time: 10 minutes
Total time: 25 minutes

Ingredients:
1 lb beef (sirloin, skirt steak, boneless short ribs...etc.)
1 to 2 heads broccoli, break into florets
2 cloves garlic, minced
2 pieces thin sliced ginger, finely chopped
Ghee or cooking fat of your choice

Beef marinade:
2 tbsp coconut aminos
1/2 tsp coarse sea salt
1 tbsp sesame oil
1/4 tsp black pepper
1 tsp arrowroot/sweet potato powder
1/4 tsp baking soda Baking soda is whole 30 friendly.
See notes section.

Sauce combo:
2 tbsp coconut aminos
1 tbsp red boat fish sauce
2 tsp sesame oil
1/4 tsp black pepper

Directions:

Slice beef into about ¼ inch thin. Marinate thin sliced beef with ingredients under "beef marinade". Mix well. Place broccoli florets in a microwave safe container. Add 1-2 tablespoons water. Loosely covered with a lid or wet paper towel and microwave for 2 minutes. Cook until broccoli is tender but still crunchy. Set aside.

Heat a wok over medium heat with 1 ½ tablespoons ghee. When hot, lower the heat to medium, add garlic and ginger.Season with a small pinch of salt and stir-fry until fragrant (about 10 seconds).

Turn up the heat to medium-high, add marinated beef. Spread beef evenly over the bottom of the saute pan and cook until the edge of the beef is slightly darkened and crispy. Do the same thing for flip slide - about ¾ way cooked through with slightly charred and crispy surface.

Add "Sauce Combo". Stir-fry about 1 minute. Add broccoli. Stir-fry another 30 seconds. Toss everything to combine.

45. EASY CROCKPOT CHICKEN STEW

Prep time: 5 minutes
Cook time: 2 hours
Total time: 2 hours 5 minutes

Ingredients:
2 cups chicken stock
2 medium carrots (1/2 cup), peeled and finely diced
2 celery sticks (1 cup), diced
½ onion (1/2 cup), diced
28 oz skinless and deboned chicken thighs diced into 1" pieces
1 spring fresh rosemary or ½ tsp dried rosemary
3 garlic cloves, minced
¼ tsp dried thyme
½ tsp dried oregano
1 cup fresh spinach
½ cup heavy cream
salt and pepper, to taste
xantham gum, to desired thickness, starting at ⅛ tsp
Directions:
Place the chicken stock, carrots, celery, onion, chicken thighs, rosemary, garlic, thyme, and oregano into a 3-quart crockpot or larger. Cook on high for 2 hours or on low for 4 hours.
Add salt and pepper, to taste.
Stir in spinach and heavy cream.

Sprinkle and thicken with xantham gum to desired thickness starting at ⅛th teaspoon. Continue to whisk until mix and cook for another 10 minutes.

46. KETO OATMEAL

Prep time: 2 minutes
Total time: 12 hours 2 minutes
You can substitute heavy whipping cream, coconut milk, and almond into any recipe. Generally you will need 75% as much almond milk as you need coconut milk or heavy cream. It's recommended to use chia seeds whenever almond milk is used to create a thicker consistency.

Ingredients:
Pumpkin Pie:
3 tbsp hemp hearts
1 tbsp 100% pumpkin puree
1/2 tsp pumpkin pie spice
1 tsp chia aeeds
2 drops liquid Stevia
3 tbsp unsweetened almond milk

Almond Joy:
3 tbsp hemp hearts
1/2 tbsp chopped almonds
1/2 tbsp Lily's Chocolate Chips
1/2 tbsp unsweetened shredded coconut
1/4 cup coconut milk
1 drop liquid Stevia

Double Chocolate:

3 tbsp hemp hearts

1 tbsp unsweetened cocoa powder

1/2 tbsp Lily's Chocolate Chips

1/4 tsp pink salt

1/4 cup heavy whipping cream

1 tsp chia seeds

2 drops liquid Stevia

Maple Walnut:

3 tbsp hemp hearts

1 tbsp walnuts, chopped

1/2 tbsp sugar-free maple syrup

1/2 tsp ground cinnamon

3 tbsp unsweetened almond milk

1 tsp chia seeds

Peanut Butter:

3 tbsp hemp hearts

1 tbsp peanut butter

1 tsp chia seeds

1 drop liquid Stevia

3 tbsp unsweetened almond milk

Broats:

3 tbsp hemp hearts

1 tbsp protein powder

1 tsp chia seeds
1/4 cup heavy whipping cream

Turmeric-Vanilla:
3 tbsp hemp hearts
1/4 cup coconut milk
1 tsp chia seeds
1/2 tsp turmeric powder
1/2 tsp vanilla extract
2 drops liquid Stevia

Directions:
Add all ingredients to a bowl or mason jar. Mix together thoroughly.
Place in the refrigerator overnight, or a minimum of 4 hours. Open the next day and enjoy!

47. LEMON THYME CHICKEN

Ingredients:
2 lb grass-fed beef or pork
1 1/2 tsp sea salt
1 tsp ground black pepper
2 large pastured eggs
1 medium onion, peeled and finely chopped
2 cups mushrooms (any kind will do), finely chopped
1/2 cup finely chopped OR grated carrots
2 loosely-packed cups of spinach, finely chopped
1 tsp dry thyme
3 cloves of garlic, peeled and minced
1 1/2 tbsp Dijon mustard

Directions:
Preheat your oven to 350 degrees F.
In a large bowl combine all of the ingredients. Using freshly washed hands, mix the ingredients until everything is blended together evenly.
Portion out the meat mixture evenly between a 12-hole muffin tin.
Bake for 25-30 minutes or until meat is cooked.
Enjoy warm with cauliflower rice, a salad, or side of choice.
Freeze leftovers or store in fridge for up to 5 days.

48. KETO PANCAKES

Total time: 20 minutes

Ingredients:
½ cup plus 1 tbsp almond flour
½ cup grass-fed cream cheese
4 eggs
½ tsp cinnamon
1 tbsp butter or avocado oil, for frying

Directions:
Mix all ingredients in a blender.
In a frying pan, over medium heat, add in the butter or oil.
Pour in 2–3 tablespoons of batter per pancake and turn over once the center begins to bubble (usually takes about 3–4 minutes).
Top with butter and cinnamon

49. KETO CHOCOLATE CHIA PUDDING

Ingredients:
1 (13.5 oz) can full-fat coconut milk, blended
1 cup water
2 tbsp cacao powder
⅛ tsp vanilla stevia
⅛ tsp Celtic sea salt
¼ cup chia seeds

Directions:
In a vitamix, combine coconut milk, water, cacao powder, stevia, and salt.
Blend until smooth.
Transfer mixture to a one quart mason jar.
Add chia seeds and shake well.
Refrigerate overnight to let chia seeds soften and absorb liquid.
Notes: For this recipe, it's important to blend the coconut milk in a high-powered blender. This way you'll have a smooth and creamy pudding, rather than one with little lumps of coconut milk in it.

50. CHEESY GARLIC CREAMED SPINACH

Total time: 5 - 10 minutes

Ingredients:
3 tbsp butter
4 cloves garlic, minced
2 lb fresh spinach leaves
sea salt and black pepper, to taste
1 cup heavy cream
1/4 cup grated Parmesan cheese
1/4 cup shredded mozzarella cheese
1/4 cup goat cheese

Directions:
In a large sauté pan over medium heat, melt the butter. Add the garlic and sauté for 1 minute, being careful not to burn it.

Add the spinach. Season with sea salt and black pepper to taste.Sauté until the spinach is wilted. Remove the spinach from the pan and let it drain. You may need to press it in a colander to remove all of the excess moisture.

To the same pan, add the heavy cream, Parmesan, mozzarella and goat cheeses. Lower the heat to low and allow the sauce to thicken, 5 to 10 minutes. Add the wilted spinach back to the pan and toss until evenly coated in the creamy cheese sauce.

51. CHICKEN IN WHITE SAUCE

Prep time: 10 minutes
Cook time: 40 minutes
Total time: 50 minutes

Ingredients:
4 chicken breasts, medium sized
1 cup coconut cream
1 cup white wine
300 g mushrooms
300 g green beans, halved
2 tsp Dijon mustard
4 cloves garlic
¼ cup olive oil
1 tsp fresh thyme, chopped
1 tsp salt
1 tsp pepper

Directions:
Preheat the oven to 355F (180C).
Heat a frying pan to medium heat with half the amount of olive oil required for the recipe, add the chicken breasts and cook each side for 2 minutes.
Place the chicken on baking tray lined with baking paper. Cook for 15 minutes.

Meanwhile, in the same frying pan, slice the mushrooms and slightly brown them using the reaining olive oil and garlic.

Add the beans, coconut cream, white wine, dijon mustard, thyme, salt and pepper. Mix around in the pan and reduce to a simmer. The sauce should be quite watery to start with, and will reduce to a lovely creamy sauce.

Once the chicken has reached 15 minutes, remove from the oven. Plate the chicken and cover with sauce, mushrooms, and beans.

52. GUILTLESS GARLIC PARMESAN WINGS

Total time: 35 minutes

Ingredients:
12 chicken wings
1½ tbsp avocado oil
1 tbsp garlic powder
½ cup parmesan, grated
½ cup pecorino romano, grated
1 tsp salt
1 tsp pepper

Directions:
Preheat oven to 350 F.
Line a baking sheet with parchment and set aside.
Mix spices and cheeses in a bowl.
Coat the wings in oil.
Dip wings in mixture.
Bake for 30 minutes.

53. EGGPLANT ROLLATINI RECIPE

Total time: 1 hour

Ingredients:
2 large eggplants, sliced lengthwise
½ tsp sea salt
½ tsp black pepper
1–1½ cups marinara sauce
2 large eggs
3 cups spinach
1 package goat feta (4 oz)
1 tsp dried oregano
1 tsp parsley
1 tsp dried basil
2 cups pecorino romano, grated
1 cup raw sheep cheese, grated

Directions:
Preheat oven to 450 F.
While your oven is heating up, cut the ends off of the two eggplants and then slice lengthwise.
Place the eggplant slices on a baking sheet lined with parchment paper and sprinkle with salt and pepper.
Bake for 12–15 minutes, remove and allow to cool.
Reduce heat to 400 F.
In a medium bowl, mix the eggs, goat cheese, spinach, oregano, parsley, basil, 1 cup pecorino

romano, ½ cup raw sheep cheese, salt and pepper, mixing until well combined.

In a 9x13 baking dish, add ¾ cup marinara.

Place ¼ cup cheese mixture onto one end of the sliced eggplant, then roll it up and transfer to baking dish, continuing until baking dish is full.

Cover with remaining marinara and cheese.

Bake for 25 minutes and allow to cool for 10 minutes before serving.

54. KETO SMOOTHIE RECIPE WITH AVOCADO, CHIA SEEDS & CACAO

Total time: 15 minutes

Ingredients:
1–1¼ cups full-fat coconut milk
½ frozen avocado
1 tbsp nut butter of choice
1 tbsp chia seeds, soaked in 3 tablespoons of water for 10 minutes
2 tsp cacao nibs, cacao powder or cocoa powder or 1 scoop of chocolate protein powder made from bone broth
1 tbsp coconut oil
ice (optional)

For topping:
cacao nibs and cinnamon
¼ cup water, if needed

Directions:
Add ingredients into a high-powered blender, processing until well-combined.
Top with cacao nibs and cinnamon.

55. LOW-CARB CAULIFLOWER POT PIES

Prep time: 15 minutes
Cook time: 25 minutes
Total time: 40 minutes

Ingredients:
Cauliflower Base:
1 medium head cauliflower (4-5 cups cauliflower rice)
1/4 cup shredded parmesan cheese
1 egg
pinch of salt and pepper

Pot Pie Filling:
1/2 onion, diced
1 1/2 cups chicken broth
1/4 cup almond milk, unsweetened
1 cup frozen mixed vegetables
8 oz cooked chicken, diced
1 tbsp onion powder
1/2 tsp salt
1/2 tsp black pepper
2 tbs cornstarch, plus 1/4 cup water

Instructions:
Preheat oven to 400° F. Add the cauliflower to the bowl of a food processor and pulse until you achieve a rice-like consistency. Transfer cauliflower "rice" to a

bowl and microwave for 5 minutes. Set aside and allow cauliflower to cool for approx 10 minutes.

Add the cauliflower rice to a cheesecloth and squeeze out as much of the juice from the cauliflower as possible. If you don't, the bases may end up soggy (the key here is to really get as much of that juice out as you can). Once you have done a round with the cheesecloth. Repeat with another dry cheesecloth to ensure you have removed a majority of the liquid.

Add the dried cauliflower rice to a bowl with the egg, parmesan cheese, salt and pepper. Using your hands, combine all of the ingredients thoroughly. Spray a large muffin pan or 4 ramekins and gently press the cauliflower mixture to the sides, creating a cauliflower bowl. Bake for 20-25 minutes or until the centers are dry and the edges are golden brown.

While the cauliflower bases are in the oven, spray a medium saucepan with cooking spray and saute the diced onion on high heat until slightly tender. Reduce heat to medium and add the chicken broth, almond milk, mixed vegetables, onion powder, salt and black pepper. Stir and cover for approx 5-8 minutes or until frozen vegetables are soft.

Mix the cornstarch with the water to make a slurry and add to the sauce with the cooked chicken. Stir in the cornstarch mixture and increase heat to high and cook until sauce begins to boil. Remove from heat.

Fill each cauliflower base with the pot pie filling and serve.

56. JALAPENO POPPERS

Total time: 25 minutes

Ingredients:
10–12 jalapeno peppers, stemmed removed, sliced in ½ length-wise and seeds removed
1 package turkey bacon (optional*)
½-1 cup goat feta
½-1 cup shredded goat cheese
½ tsp cumin
½ tsp chili powder
½ tsp smoked paprika
½ tsp oregano
salt and pepper to taste

Directions:
Preheat oven to 350 F.
Line a baking sheet, or two, with parchment paper and set aside.
In a medium-sized bowl add everything except the jalapeños and turkey bacon, mixing until well-combined.
Using your hands, fill each halved jalapeño with the cheese mixture.
Wrap jalapeno with turkey bacon and place on baking sheet.
Bake for 20 minutes.
Pair with our Avocado Ranch Dressing.

57. KETO LOW-CARB GRANOLA CEREAL

Prep time: 10 minutes
Cook time: 15 minutes
Total time: 25 minutes

Ingredients:
1 cup almonds
1 cup hazelnuts
1 cup pecans
1/3 cup pumpkin seeds
1/3 cup sunflower seeds
6 tbsp Erythritol
1/2 cup golden flaxseed meal
1 large egg white
1/4 cup butter (measured solid, then melted; can use coconut oil or ghee for dairy-free)
1 tsp vanilla extract

Directions:
Preheat oven to 325° F. Line a large baking sheet, or two small ones, with parchment paper.
Pulse almonds and hazelnuts in a food processor intermittently, until most of the nuts are in chopped into large pieces (about 1/4 to 1/2 of the full size of the nuts).

Add the pecans. Pulse again, stopping when the pecans are in large pieces (pecans are added later since they are softer).

Add the pumpkin seeds, sunflower seeds, erythritol, and golden flaxseed meal. Pulse just until everything is mixed well. Don't over-process! You want to have plenty of nut pieces remaining, and most of the seeds should be intact.

Add the egg white to the food processor. Whisk together the melted butter and vanilla extract in a small bowl, and evenly pour that in, too.

Pulse a couple times, mix a little from the bottom toward the top with a spatula, then pulse a couple times again. Repeat as needed until everything is coated evenly. Again, avoid over-processing. At the end of this step, you'll have a combination of coarse meal and nut pieces, and everything should be a little damp from the egg white and butter.

Transfer the nut mixture to the prepared baking sheet in a uniform layer, pressing together into a thin rectangle (about 1/4 to 1/3 in (.6-.8 cm) thick). Bake for 15-18 minutes, until lightly browned, especially at the edges.

Cool completely before breaking apart into pieces (the granola will be soft when you remove it from the oven, but will crisp up as it cools).

58. KETO ZUCCHINI BREAD WITH WALNUTS

Ingredients:
3 large eggs
½ cup olive oil
1 tsp vanilla extract
2 ½ cups almond flour
1 ½ cups erythritol
½ tsp salt
1 ½ tsp baking powder
½ tsp nutmeg
1 tsp ground cinnamon
¼ tsp ground ginger
1 cup grated zucchini
½ cup chopped walnuts

Directions:
Preheat oven to 350°F. Whisk together the eggs, oil, and vanilla extract. Set to the side.
In another bowl, mix together the almond flour, erythritol, salt, baking powder, nutmeg, cinnamon, and ginger. Set to the side.
Using a cheesecloth or paper towel, take the zucchini and squeeze out the excess water.
Then, whisk the zucchini into the bowl with the eggs.
Slowly add the dry ingredients into the egg mixture using a hand mixer until fully blended.

Lightly spray a 9×5 loaf pan, and spoon in the zucchini bread mixture.

Then, spoon in the chopped walnuts on top of the zucchini bread. Press walnuts into the batter using a spatula.

Bake for 60-70 minutes at 350°F or until the walnuts on top look browned.

59. KETO WALNUT BREAD

Ingredients:
3 large eggs
½ cup olive oil
1 tsp vanilla extract
2 1/2 cups almond flour
1 1/2 cups erythritol
½ tsp salt
1 1/2 tsp baking powder
½ tsp nutmeg
1 tsp ground cinnamon
¼ tsp ground ginger
1 cup grated zucchini
½ cup chopped walnuts

Directions:
Preheat oven to 350°F. Whisk together the eggs, oil, and vanilla extract. Set to the side.
In another bowl, mix together the almond flour, erythritol, salt, baking powder, nutmeg, cinnamon, and ginger. Set to the side.
Using a cheesecloth or paper towel, take the zucchini and squeeze out the excess water.
Then, whisk the zucchini into the bowl with the eggs.
Slowly add the dry ingredients into the egg mixture using a hand mixer until fully blended.

Lightly spray a 9x5 loaf pan, and spoon in the zucchini bread mixture.

Then, spoon in the chopped walnuts on top of the zucchini bread. Press walnuts into the batter using a spatula.

Bake for 60-70 minutes at 350°F or until the walnuts on top look browned.

60. LOW-CARB TORTILLA CHIPS

Prep time: 10 minutes
Cook time: 10 minutes
Total time: 20 minutes

Ingredients:
2 cups almond flour
1/2 tsp chili powder
1/2 tsp garlic powder
1/2 tsp cumin
1/4 tsp paprika
1/4 tsp sea salt
1 large egg, beaten
1/2 cup mozzarella cheese, shredded

Directions:
Preheat the oven to 350° F . Line a baking sheet with parchment paper.

In a large bowl, mix together the almond flour and spices.

Add the egg and mix using a hand mixer, until a crumbly dough forms.

In a small bowl, microwave the mozzarella until it's melted and easy to stir (alternatively, you can melt it using a double broiler on the stove). Add to the dough mixture and knead/squeeze with your hands until well incorporated. If it stops incorporating before it's fully mixed, you can reheat it for 15-20 seconds again before kneading more.

Place the dough between two large pieces of parchment paper. Use a rolling pin to roll out very thin, about 1/16 in (2 mm) thick.

Cut the dough into triangles and arranged on the parchment lined baking sheet. Bake for 8-12 minutes, until golden and firm. The chips may release some sizzling oil on the top - just pat dry with a paper towel. They will crisp up as they cool.

61. PUMPKIN SPICE KETO FAT BOMB RECIPE

Prep time: 10 minutes

Ingredients:
1/2 cup coconut oil
3/4 cup pumpkin puree
1/3 cup golden flax
1 tsp cinnamon or I used 2 drops cinnamon bark vitality essential oil
1/2 tsp nutmeg
1/4 tsp sea salt
1/4 cup confectioner's Swerve or 1/3 tsp stevia or to taste

Directions:
Mix all the ingredients in a bowl and place in the freezer for 30 minutes. Roll into balls and place on a plate. Let the balls sit in the refrigerator for 1 hours before eating. Keeps for a week or longer in the freezer.

62. EASY CHEESY ZUCCHINI GRATIN

Ingredients:
4 cups sliced raw zucchini
1 small onion, peeled and sliced thin
salt and pepper to taste
1 1/2 cups shredded pepper jack cheese
2 tbsp butter
1/2 tsp garlic powder
1/2 cup heavy whipping cream

Instructions:
Preheat oven to 375° F.
Grease a 9×9 or equivalent oven-proof pan.
Overlap 1/3 of the zucchini and onion slices in the pan, then season with salt and pepper and sprinkle with 1/2 cup of shredded cheese.
Repeat two more times until you have three layers and have used up all of the zucchini, onions, and shredded cheese.
Combine the garlic powder, butter, and heavy cream in a microwave safe dish.
Heat for one minute or until the butter has melted. Stir.
Gently pour the butter and cream mixture over the zucchini layers.
Bake at 375° F for about 45 minutes, or until the liquid has thickened and the top is golden brown.
Serve warm.

63. KETO SNACKS

Total time: 25 minutes

Ingredients:
4–6 eggs
1 avocado
¼ tsp sea salt
¼ tsp pepper
¼ tsp garlic
¼ tsp chili powder
¼ tsp cumin
¼ tsp smoked paprika, optional*
2 tbsp cilantro

Directions:
In a medium pot, add eggs and cover with water until fully submerged.
Bring to a boil, then remove from heat and cover for 12–13 minutes.
Fill a large bowl with ice water and, using a slotted spoon, gently place eggs in the bowl, allowing eggs to chill for 5 minutes.
Remove outer casing from eggs and slice in half lengthwise, removing the yolk.
Add the yolk, along with the avocado and spices to a bowl, mixing together until well combined.
Add the mixture to the egg halves.
Drizzle with lime juice and top with cilantro.

64. BLACKBERRY-NUT FAT BOMBS

Ingredients:
2 oz macadamia nuts, crushed
4 oz neufchatel cheese (cream cheese)
1 cup blackberries
3 tbsp mascarpone cheese
1 cup coconut oil
1 cup coconut butter
1/2 tsp vanilla extract
1/2 tsp lemon juice
stevia to taste

Directions:
Crush the macadamia nuts and press into the bottom of a baking dish or mold. Bake 5 to 7 minutes at 325 F, or until golden brown.
Remove from the oven and allow to cool slightly.
Spread a layer of softened cream cheese over the nut "crust."
In a bowl, mix together blackberries, mascarpone cheese, coconut oil, coconut butter, vanilla, lemon juice and sweetener (optional) until smooth.
Pour mixture over the cream cheese layer. Freeze for 30 minutes to an hour. Remove and store in the fridge.

65. BUFFALO KETO CHICKEN TENDERS

Prep time: 10 minutes
Cook time: 30 minutes
Total time: 40 minutes

Ingredients:
1 lb chicken breast tenders
1 cup almond flour
1 large egg
1 tbsp heavy whipping cream
6 oz Buffalo sauce
salt & pepper

Instructions:
Preheat oven to 350°.
Season chicken tenders with salt and pepper. Season the almond flour generously with salt and pepper.
Beat 1 egg together with 1 tablespoon of heavy cream.
Dip each tender first in the egg wash and then into the seasoned almond flour. We like to place the tenders in a Tupperware container with the almond flour and shake to coat. A Ziploc bag also works well.
Place tenders on a lightly greased baking sheet. Bake for 30 minutes. If they are not as crispy as you would like you can additionally broil them for 2-3 minutes.

Allow tenders to cool for 5 minutes and then place them in a tupperware container, add the buffalo sauce and shake to coat. Gently shaking is best to prevent the batter from falling off.

66. COCONUT KETO MILK

Prep time: 2 minutes
Cook time: 3 minutes
Total time: 5 minutes

Ingredients:
½ cup filtered water
½ cup coconut milk
2 tbsp unsalted butter (grass-fed)
1 tbsp coconut oil or MCT oil
2 tbsp unsweetened cocoa powder
¼ tsp vanilla extract
dash cinnamon
1-2 teaspoons Erythritol –(optional)

Directions:
In a medium sized pot (if using hand blender) or a small pot (if using blender), bring water and coconut milk to a boil.
Remove from heat.
Add the rest of the ingredients into the coconut milk and water.
Blend using a hand blender (like the ones for soups) or pour the mixture into a blender and blend till frothy.

67. KETO CHEESE MEATBALLS

Prep time: 10 minutes
Cook time: 10 minutes
Total time: 20 minutes

Ingredients:
500 g ground beef
100 g cheese, mozzarella works best, but cheddar is fine
3 tbsp Parmesan cheese
1 tsp garlic Powder
1/2 tsp salt
1/2 tsp pepper

Directions:
Cut the cheese into cubes (1cm by 1cm).
Mix the dry ingredients with the ground beef.
Wrap the cubes of cheese in the meat (500g should make about 9 balls).
Pan fry the meatballs (cover with a lid to capture the heat all around). Fingers crossed the cheese doesn't spill.

68. COCONUT BOOSTERS RECIPE

Total time: 65 minutes

Ingredients:
1 cup coconut oil
1/2 cup chia seeds
1 tsp vanilla extract
1 tbsp honey
1/4 cup unsweetened coconut flakes

Directions:
Using a hand mixer, combine all ingredients together in a bowl.
Spoon into muffin cups/muffin tins and freeze for an hour.
Sprinkle with extra coconut flakes if desired.

69. BAKED MEATBALLS RECIPE

Total time: 15 minutes

Ingredients:
1 lb beef
½ lb of both: lamb and bison
⅓ cup raw, smoked goat cheese
¼ cup of: fresh parsley, fresh basil and oregano, all finely chopped
1-2 tbsp melted coconut oil
1 tsp sea salt
1 tsp pepper
1 tsp onion powder
2 eggs
1 tbsp cassava flour

Directions:
Preheat oven to 375 F.
Line two baking sheets with parchment paper and set aside.
Add all ingredients to a large bowl and, using your hands, mix until well combined.
Roll into small meatballs and place on baking sheets.
Bake for 12-15 minutes or until internal temperature reaches 165 F.

70. GOAT CHEESE & ARTICHOKE DIP RECIPE

Total time: 5 minutes

Ingredients:
14-oz can artichoke hearts, drained
1 lb chévre goat cheese
2 tbsp olive oil
2 tsp lemon juice
1 garlic clove, minced
½ cup pecorino romano, grated
1 tbsp parsley
1 tsp chives
½ tbsp basil
½ tsp sea salt
½ tsp black pepper
Dash of cayenne pepper (optional)

Directions:
In a food processor, mix all ingredients except the pecorino romano until well incorporated and creamy. Top with freshly-grated pecorino romano.

71. LOW-CARB INDIAN SAMOSAS

Prep time: 25 minutes
Cook time: 17 minutes
Total time: 37 minutes

Ingredients:
1 tbsp butter preferably grass-fed
6 oz cauliflower finely chopped
1 medium onion, about 4 oz
3/4 tsp salt (or to taste)
1 tbsp fresh ginger root, minced
1/2 tsp coriander ground
1 tsp garam masala ground
1 tsp cumin ground
1/4 tsp cumin seeds whole
1/8-1/4 tsp red chili flakes
1/4 cup fresh cilantro chopped

Dough:
3/4 cup super-fine almond flour
1/4 tsp cumin
1/2 tsp salt
8 oz part-skim mozzarella cheese, finely shredded

Directions:
For the filling:

Preheat a large skillet over medium heat. Add butter. When butter has melted and stopped foaming, add the cauliflower and onions.

Sprinkle the salt over the vegetables.Cook, stirring occasionally, until the edges have started to brown and the vegetables are cooked through.

Stir in ginger root, coriander, garam masala, ground cumin, cumin seeds, and chili flakes. Stir for 1-2 minutes to allow the spices to toast. Turn off the heat.

Stir in the cilantro. Taste and adjust seasoning. Add salt to taste.

Preheat oven to 375° F. Have a rolling pin, 2 pieces of parchment, and a baking sheet available.

For the dough:

Set up a double boiler. I use a large sauce pan with about 1 1/2-2 inches of water in it and a medium mixing bowl that fits on top.

Bring the water in the lower part of the double boiler to a simmer over high heat. Once it is simmering, turn heat to low.

Meanwhile, place the almond flour, cumin, salt, and mozzarella in the top part of the double boiler. Stir together.

Place the bowl containing the almond flour mixture over the simmering water. Be careful not to burn yourself with the hot bowl or with steam escaping. I use a silicone mitten to hold the bowl.

Stirring the mixture constantly, heat until the mozzarella cheese melts and the mixture forms a dough.

Turn the dough out onto one of the pieces of parchment and knead a few times to equally distribute the ingredients. Shape the dough into a thick rectangle and cover with the second sheet of parchment. Roll dough into a rectangle about 8 inches wide by 16 inches long.

Cut the dough rectangle in half lengthwise, then in half cross-wise. Then cut each of the four sections in half crosswise to form 8 four-inch squares.

To assemble:

Spoon the filling onto the center of each square, dividing it equally among the squares. Fold the squares on the diagonal to form triangles and pinch the edges closed. Place one of the pieces of parchment used to roll out the dough onto a baking sheet, then place the samosas on the sheet.

Make fork holes in each samosa to provide a place for steam to release. Bake for 14-17 minutes or until golden-brown.

72. CHOCOLATE AVOCADO PUDDING

Total time: 5 minutes

Ingredients:
1/4 cup unsweetened cocoa powder
1 medium avocado
10 drops liquid Stevia
1/2 tsp vanilla extract
1 tsp pink salt

Directions:
Remove the pit from the avocado and place in a mixing bowl.

Add cocoa powder, stevia, and vanilla extract and mix with a fork until a pudding is formed. You can gently use a hand mixer also, but a fork does the job.

Top with pink sea salt.

73. LOADED HASSELBACK ZUCCHINI

Prep time: 10 minutes
Cook time: 15 minutes
Total time: 25 minutes

Ingredients:
3 medium zucchini squash
about 6-8 oz of your favorite cheese
3-4 tbsp sour cream
3 slices of crumbled cooked bacon
2-3 tbsp chopped green onion
salt and pepper, to taste

Notes: For this recipe you can use sliced cheese (pre-sliced or sliced fresh off the block) or shredded cheese. Both work great, but I find using slices the easiest. I cut my slices off the block, then cut each slice in half. You can even skip the stuffing portion altogether and whisk together a simple nacho-style cheddar cheese sauce to pour over each zucchini. Anything goes when it comes to cheese.

Directions:
Preheat oven to 425° F.
Wash and dry zucchini, and slice off the ends.
Line up a chopstick on both sides of the squash and slice until you hit the stick.

Start at one end and keep slicing into discs (granted - connected discs since we don't want to cut all the way through the squash) until you've reached the other end. Repeat for remaining squash.

Resist the urge to play the zucchini accordion-style when you're done.

Slice each zucchini in half so you have 6 mini hasselbacks.

Line a baking sheet with foil, then arrange your zukes on top.

Next, stuff cheese between each tasty little zucchini disc.

Season with salt and pepper if desired and top with another sheet of foil.

Pinch along the sides to make a foil pouch.

The foil pouch will not only help the zucchini cook quicker by steaming the squash, but will also keep the cheese melty and prevent it from browning.

Bake at 425° F for 15-20 minutes.

Allow to rest/steam covered in foil for an additional 5.

Top with sour cream, bacon, and green onion and dig in.

74. GUILTLESS GARLIC PARMESAN WINGS

Total time: 35 minutes

Ingredients:
12 chicken wings
1½ tbsp avocado oil
1 tbsp garlic powder
½ cup parmesan, grated
½ cup pecorino romano, grated
1 tsp salt
1 tsp pepper

Directions:
Preheat oven to 350 F.
Line a baking sheet with parchment and set aside.
Mix spices and cheeses in a bowl.
Coat the wings in oil.
Dip wings in mixture.
Bake for 30 minutes.

75. EGGPLANT ROLLATINI RECIPE

Total time: 1 hour

Ingredients:
2 large eggplants, sliced lengthwise
½ tsp sea salt
½ tsp black pepper
1–1½ cups marinara sauce
2 large eggs
3 cups spinach
1 package goat feta (4 oz)
1 tsp dried oregano
1 tsp parsley
1 tsp dried basil
2 cups pecorino romano, grated
1 cup raw sheep cheese, grated

Directions:
Preheat oven to 450 F.
While the oven is heating up, cut the ends off of the two eggplants and then slice lengthwise.
Place the eggplant slices on a baking sheet lined with parchment paper and sprinkle with salt and pepper.
Bake for 12–15 minutes, remove and allow to cool.
Reduce heat to 400 F.
In a medium bowl, mix the eggs, goat cheese, spinach, oregano, parsley, basil, 1 cup pecorino

romano, ½ cup raw sheep cheese, salt and pepper, mixing until well combined.

In a 9x13 baking dish, add ¾ cup marinara.

Place ¼ cup cheese mixture onto one end of the sliced eggplant, then roll it up and transfer to baking dish, continuing until baking dish is full.

Cover with remaining marinara and cheese.

Bake for 25 minutes and allow to cool for 10 minutes before serving

76. MEATBALLS

Prep time: 15 minutes
Cook time: 15 minutes
Total time: 30 minutes

Ingredients:
1/4 cup grated Parmesan cheese
1/4 cup golden flaxseed meal
1 tbsp Italian seasoning
3/4 tsp sea salt
1/2 tsp black pepper
1/4 cup unsweetened coconut milk beverage (or any milk of choice)
3 tbsp onion, grated
1 large egg
3 cloves garlic, minced
2 tbsp fresh parsley chopped
1 lb ground beef
3/4 cup marinara sauce

Directions:
Preheat the oven to 425° F. Line a baking sheet with parchment paper or foil (grease if using foil).
In a large bowl, stir together the grated Parmesan cheese, golden flaxseed meal, Italian seasoning, sea salt, and black pepper.

Whisk in the milk, grated onion, egg, garlic, and fresh parsley. Let the mixture sit for a couple of minutes.

Mix in the ground beef using your hands, until just incorporated (don't over-mix to avoid tough meatballs).

Form the mixture into 1-inch balls and place on the lined baking sheet (a small cookie scoop works well for this. If using your hands, use a gentle touch and don't pack the meatballs too tightly).

Bake for 10-12 minutes, until the meatballs are barely done (if you want them more golden, you can place them under the broiler for a couple of minutes).

Top each meatball with marinara sauce. Return to the oven and bake for 3-5 minutes, until the sauce is hot and meatballs are cooked through. Garnish with additional fresh parsley.

HOW TO STORE FOOD SAFELY AND PREVENT FOODBORNE ILLNESSES

Some foods are more susceptible to harmful pathogens than others, like milk and dairy products, eggs, beef, pork, lamb, poultry, fish, shellfish, baked potatoes, cooked rice, sprouts, sliced melons, cut melons, untreated garlic, and oil mixtures and many, many more.

Prevention of foodborne illnesses should be a primary focus of every kitchen in America. Each year, millions of people get sick from unsafe foods and over 30% of the suspected cases of foodborne illness happens at home.

Here are the five most common risk factors causing foodborne illnesses as identified by the CDC (Centers for Disease Control):

1. Purchasing food from unsafe food sources.

2. Failing to cook food adequately.

3. Holding food at incorrect temperatures.

4. Using contaminated equipment.

5. Practicing poor personal hygiene.

You can help to keep your holiday foods safe by controlling FAT TOM. What is FAT TOM? FAT TOM is the six conditions in which pathogens grow. Taking care of these six conditions helps prevent outbreaks of foodborne illnesses.

F = Food. Pathogens need a source of energy.

A = Acidity. Foods that contain little or no acidity are where pathogens grown best.

T = Temperature. Pathogens grow best in food held between 41°F and 135°F. This is known as the "danger zone."

T = time. Pathogens need time to grow. After four hours, food left in the danger zone will grow a high enough legal of pathogens to make someone sick.

O = Oxygen. Some pathogens need oxygen to grow while some others grow where there is no oxygen.

M = Moisture. Pathogens need moisture in food to grow.

As you can see, these items are easy to follow. Become familiar with these tips and use your new knowledge to keep food safe and thereby help to keep your family and guests safe.

When you are thinking about starting a long-term food storage program, there many things to consider.

First off, what are your food storage goals? A common guideline is to start with a three-month supply of foods you normally eat, and then build up a one-year supply of longer-term foods.

What IS long-term food storage? This concept is basically to have a supply of food that can sustain your family for one year in case of a long-lasting emergency situation. These bulk foods tend to have long shelf lives and when combined with a few other ingredients can make a wide variety of meals. Some of the most common foods stored are wheat, oats, rice, legumes, powdered milk, oil, salt, yeast, etc. Basically the staple foods of any diet.

How much should you store? While there are basic food storage calculators out there to help you along the way, they aren't necessarily exactly right for every situation. Here are some do's and don'ts that can help you as you get started with your family's personal plan.

Food Storage Do's:

- DO get a partner to work with you, share ideas, and motivate you.

- DO learn how to actually USE the foods that you are storing.

- DO buy the necessary kitchen appliances to help you use the foods.

- DO include the foods you store as part of your everyday cooking.

- DO be adventurous and try new recipes.

- DO start small and work your way up to a full year supply.

- DO make sure to have an emergency plan in place.

- DO expand your food storage to include other things once you get the basics down.

- DO educate yourself in other aspects of emergency preparedness such as alternative heating/cooking methods.

Food Storage Don'ts:

- DON'T get overwhelmed and just give up completely.

- DON'T store foods that your family hates just because the calculator says to.

- DON'T think that cooking with these foods is fattening and unhealthy.

- DON'T think that using bulk foods and cooking from scratch is really inconvenient.

- DON'T get too crazy about figuring out how to cook without electricity when you are just getting started.

- DON'T buy everything all at once and kill your budget.

- DON'T try to get your family to change their diet completely over night.

- DON'T be too anxious to buy things that you don't wait for good sales.

- DON'T focus too much on long-term items and neglect to store some basic foods you use on a regular basis.